ACADEMIC
WOMEN

ACADEMIC WOMEN

Working Towards Equality

Angela Simeone

BERGIN & GARVEY PUBLISHERS, INC.
MASSACHUSETTS

First published in 1987 by
Bergin & Garvey Publishers, Inc.
670 Amherst Road
South Hadley, Massachusetts 01075

789   987654321

Printed in the United States of America

Library of Congress Cataloging-in-Publication Data

Simeone, Angela.
  Academic women.

  Bibliography: p. 145
  Includes index.
  1. Women college teachers—United States.   2. College teachers'
socioeconomic status—United States   3. Sex discrimination in
education—United States.   I. Title.
LB2332.3.S56 1987   378'.12'088042   86-26436
ISBN 0-89789-111-2
ISBN 0-89789-114-7 (pbk.)

To my family

Contents

vii

Acknowledgments

At the end of four years of work on this book, there are many people who have my heartfelt appreciation and gratitude.

I am grateful to Jim Bergin for his support, encouragement, and enthusiasm. Michelle Fine has been a great source of intellectual and personal inspiration, and her insightful comments have added immeasurably to the quality of this work. Special thanks go to David Webster for his good advice and suggestions.

I am indebted to Jessie Bernard for the enormous contribution of her work, Academic Women, and for generously consenting to write the Foreword to this book. In addition, my gratitude goes to the faculty women who shared with me their personal histories, which served as inspiration and brought life and energy to my work.

I must also acknowledge my many friends and colleagues, especially Debbie Phillips, Jan Folkertsma, and Jeff Onore, whose encouragement sustained me through this four-year adventure. I am grateful to Andy Friedland, not only for his computer assistance, but for the boost I received from his enthusiasm. I will forever be indebted to Ben Yagoda for editorial help, intellectual debate, gentle prodding, and—most important—wonderful fun and friendship.

Finally, this book is a gift to my family, for their boundless interest, involvement, and pride in my work.

Foreword

The author of this book begins with the question: "To what extent have attempts to achieve equity for faculty women in higher education been effective?" (3) She concludes that "while there has certainly been some improvement in the conditions they face, the overall picture remains basically unchanged" (141). Addressing the same question — "fair science" — some seven years ago, Jonathan Cole had concluded that "attempts to achieve equity" for academic women had been effective at some periods of time but not so in others (1979, 223).[1] Thus, he tells us, "feminist activity in the 1920s did reduce discrimination on the basis of sex at least in the high-prestige academic departments" (223). Unfortunately, however, this trend toward equity was reversed in the 1930s and not resumed until the 1960s. The net result of these fluctuations was, apparently, that overall there was not much change. For academia is not an island unto itself but part of a widely ramifying economic and political system which may help or hinder the achievement of equity at different times.

Nor is activism itself a standardized entity the same always and everywhere. Sometimes the emphasis of activism falls on the women themselves, on what they can do for themselves. Sometimes it is on the institutions where change is sought. Illustrative of the first is a *Handbook for Women Scholars* published in 1982 with the subtitle, *Strategies for Success.*[2] The other is addressed to academic administrators. It is, in fact, "a basic reference tool for presidents, vice presidents for academic affairs, deans of students, trustees and other concerned members of the administration, faculty, and staff" (x).[3] With so much effort being invested in the assault on discrim-

xi

ination, it seems unlikely that the overall situation can remain "basically unchanged" for a great deal longer.

But there are other ways to measure the position of academic women than the standard ones of numbers, salaries, and tenure, and Dr. Simeone does not limit her discussion to the standard ones. By Chapter 3 she turns to trends that project a quite different picture. For the really important news about academic women in the last two decades is not so much what has been or not been done to or for them in terms of salary, promotion, or tenure as it is the enormous contribution women have been making to the fundamental role of academia, the creation of knowledge. Dr. Simeone leads up to this point by way of the discussion on interpersonal relationships (Chapter 4), especially of the fundamental impact of networks that have been burgeoning so rapidly in recent years.

> These networks are not a reaction and a second-best alternative to women's exclusion from male networks, but rather speak to the positive valuing by women of each other's work, experience, and support. In fact there are some who would argue that these networks constitute the most vital development within the recent history of American higher education, and that this shift in centrality has opened institutions and disciplines to new and exciting dimensions in scholarship, curriculum, methodology, and practice (99).

I am among those who believe these networks are, indeed, a vital development, that they have, indeed, opened up "new and exciting dimensions in scholarship." They have helped in making it possible for more and more academic women to become innovative "women-of-knowledge" (Chapter 3). Their mutual support has emboldened women to "challenge the status quo and battle active or passive resistance to get . . . [their] ideas to the forefront" (53).

The result has been what I have called The Feminist Enlightenment which has proved to be well-nigh revolutionary. I have compared the feminists who initiated it beginning in the late 60s and 70s to the *philosophes* of the French Enlightenment. Like them, these women wrote, discussed, published. The stream of books, pamphlets, articles, monographs, that have issued from their typewriters and word processors has been spectacular. The effect of these words, shaped and sharpened by their increasing mastery of research

— itself one of the most important arrows in the feminist quiver[4]
— was like the storming of the Bastille or "the shot heard round
the world." Academia will never be the same again.

> For the hunger for knowledge about the female world had
> become voracious. "Women's Studies," courses in uni-
> versities became insatiable. All angles of the female world
> were eagerly explored. . . . Provision was increasingly
> being made on all kinds of programs for research studies
> dealing with women. . . . This research push was one of
> the most important aspects — as antecedent and as con-
> sequence — of the Feminist Enlightenment. It was a long
> step toward female empowerment. Women were learn-
> ing how to use the growing armory of research technol-
> ogy. . . . and how to ask relevant questions. They were
> no longer to be in the vulnerable position vis-a-vis the
> male world of having to receive the male canon as un-
> impeachable. The sociology of science was showing them
> how to conceptualize their problems. This training in
> scientific research was to prove one of the most important
> trends on the current world scene. It rendered possible
> the autonomous participation of women in the creation
> of knowledge not only about their own world but also
> about the male world. . . . With training, they developed
> the skills for asking their own questions, mapping their
> own reality, formulating their own paradigms, making
> their own interpretations, for handling their own archives
> and documentation. In brief, for using the tools of research
> to make their own discoveries about themselves, who
> they were, what they did. . . . (Bernard, 1986).[5]

Unlike the situation one sees when looking at the last two decades
in terms of standard measures, the situation as seen from this perspective is far from unchanged.

True, there is a lot left to do on the way to equity for women in
academia. But in the meanwhile in many academic disciplines
women are creating new paradigms, producing new data, expanding
knowledge, pushing back the boundaries of ignorance. The sheer
volume of all this scholarly productivity must surely in time reach
the male academic realm. This book catches the processes at work
in the Feminist Enlightenment. It describes the way different
women have responded to it. Some have welcomed the new para-

digms it has generated. They were glad to have the new vocabulary that made it possible for them to name and thus render visible some of the more subtle forms of discrimination — condescension, innuendo, exclusion, body language — of which it was so hard to convince people without adequate vocabulary and research. There were some who resisted the Enlightenment, they still blamed the victim — if you're good enough you will succeed — and some who also rejected identification with women, and even, or especially, feminism (Chapter 4).

Still, there seem to be enough academic women who recognize the importance and value of the Feminist Enlightenment and hope that it will reach more and more academic men. The author cherishes such a hope:

> As the number of women in academia increases, there will almost necessarily be an accompanying increase in informal interaction between men and women, which should help break down myths, stereotypes, and barriers (. . . .). [Only then] will women truly have access to the same institutional support as men, and . . . academia will be enriched by the benefit of women's fullest participation (99–100).
>
> JESSIE BERNARD

1. Jonathan Cole, *Fair Science Women in the Scientific Community*, New York: Free Press, 1979.
2. Mary L. Spencer, Monika Kehoe, and Karen Speece, *Handbook for Women Scholars, Strategies for Success*, San Francisco: Americas Behavioral Research Corporation, 1982. This book includes the names of 51 advocacy organizations, 50 professional caucuses and committees, 33 research and resource centers, and a "survival guide" which includes how to use Title IX, how to file a faculty grievance, 24 career, financial, and legal resources.
3. Karen Bogart, *Toward Equity: An Action Manual for Women in Academe*, Washington, D.C.: Project on the Status and Education of Women, Association of American Colleges. This project includes a description of almost 150 programs and policies that promote equity for women in the academic community and that are adaptable to other institutions. The assumption is that the achievement of equality is a given and that the problem is to find ways to bring it about.
4. Jessie Bernard, *The Female World from a Global Perspective*, Bloomington, Indiana: Indiana University Press, 1986.
5. Ibid.

Introduction

Before turning to the major topic of concern here—a brief overview of where academic women stand at the beginning of the decade—let me strike an optimistic note: all our efforts, all our activities, all our undertakings do make a difference. Slow and discouraging as the pace may seem, our activism does count.

—Jessie Bernard (1982)

Yet all the arguments, the excuses, the myths, the adamant refusals to take affirmative action toward establishing equity do not change the fact that sex discrimination is perhaps the most serious problem in higher education today. It is serious because it cuts out or it cuts down fifty percent of the potential competition for university jobs and therefore lowers the quality of university teaching and research. In the name of excellence, women are effectively frozen out of higher education. In the name of excellence, it is excellence which suffers.

—Joan Abramson (1975)

The past twenty years have been important ones with respect to the status of women in American society. The contemporary women's movement, beginning in the mid-1960s, introduced the notion of sexism to the general population. Since then, women and men have challenged longstanding and pervasive inequities in occupational, economic, political, and social status. It is now widely acknowledged that women, to one degree or another, have been the victims of individual and institutional discriminatory attitudes and practices based on their sex. With this societal change came change in the lives of individuals. As women ventured into traditionally

1

male terrain they became more free of the constraints of the repro-
ductive process and examined their own experiences and behavior
in a new light.

The issue of sexism in general, and of sexism within higher education in particular, has been the focus of considerable attention.
Many within academia would say that slowly, but surely, women
are beginning to achieve a place of significance within American
higher education. Those who resist stronger affirmative action efforts claim that women have already achieved equality, or even a
place of privilege and preference. Yet many feminists, both male
and female, contend that any progress which has been made is, in
the final analysis, superficial, and inconsequential.

In attempting to determine which view is closest to the truth, it is
essential to start with the works of Jessie Bernard. Bernard has had
a long and distinguished career in academia. Born in 1903, she received her B.A. in 1923 and her M.A. one year later from the University of Minnesota, and her Ph.D. from Washington University in
1935. She is currently Research Scholar, *Honoris Causa*, at Pennsylvania State University. She has published more than fifteen
books, including *The Sex Game, Women and the Public Interest*,
and *The Female World*, and articles on a wide range of subjects.

In 1964, Bernard published *Academic Women*, which was a full-
scale description of the status of women in academia in 1964. Uti-
lizing current research and her own observations, she wrote about
the ways in which the system supported prejudice against women,
about the ways in which women undercut themselves, about the
role anomalies and confusion faced by both men and women, about
the impact of husband and family on women's careers, and about
how women fared on measures such as salary, rank, employment,
and graduate school attendance. Throughout her analysis, she demonstrated an abiding respect for the contributions academic women
had made and an appreciation of the difficulties and barriers which
they faced.

In the twenty-two years since *Academic Women* was published,
the contemporary women's movement has come to the fore, bringing with it highly touted changes in attitudes, behaviors, and institutions. Colleges and universities have been a specific focus of
the more general attempt to achieve equity for women in society.
Indeed, the status of faculty women in higher education is an especially important issue, since faculty members serve as role models

for young women and men at a critical stage of their lives. In addition, so much of how we view the world, as a society, comes from the learning and scholarship derived from institutions of higher learning. Insofar as women are excluded from creating and disseminating knowledge, an incomplete, indeed harmful, picture of the world is painted.

What has been the real progress of women in academia in the two decades since *Academic Women* was published? To what extent have attempts to achieve equity for faculty women in higher education been effective? In what ways has institutional sexism had an impact on their experiences and opportunities? This study will suggest some answers to these questions.

In doing so, I have attempted to replicate the method used by Jessie Bernard in *Academic Women*—presenting a wide variety of studies pertaining directly or indirectly to faculty women and then suggesting larger trends indicated by the findings. In addition, to illustrate the ways in which these trends are played out in the lives of individuals, I conducted interviews with twenty female faculty members at a large, prestigious, northeastern research university, at which women made up 14.5 percent of the standing faculty at the time of this study. Of those interviewed, seventeen were white (all but one American born) and three were black. Eight were assistant professors, eight were associate professors, and four were full professors; eleven had tenure. They represented a wide range of schools and disciplines: American studies, biology, dental hygiene, education, engineering, English, marketing, medicine, nursing, regional science, romance languages, social work, and sociology. I asked the faculty women to describe their own careers, focusing on the advantages and disadvantages they felt they faced as women in academia. Each interview included questions on major interests and influences, treatment from faculty and students, friendships and networks, identification with other women and women's issues, special conflicts or ambivalences, perceived power and influence, and the impact of marital status and children on their careers. My aim was to use these experiences, and the quotations from published autobiographical accounts of academic women at other institutions, to bring the data to life. I believe they do so.

The story of women in higher education comprises far more than facts and figures on participation rates, hiring, salary, and other quantifiable measures, although they bring with them clear and important messages. Equally important are the subtle, and often not so subtle, processes which lead to the quantitative data. This work will attempt to describe both.

Chapter 1 investigates those factors which lead women to choose, or to be discouraged from choosing, academic careers. Chapter 2 assesses how they have fared on measures which are commonly considered indicators of status—institutional affiliation, salary, rank, and tenure. Chapter 3 is an analysis of the faculty role itself, and the differences between women and men in the way that they play it. Chapters 4 and 5 examine informal interaction in the academic setting, and how women fare in collegial and mentoring relationships. The impact of women's marital and family status on their careers, with a particular focus on institutional supports and barriers to reconciling domestic and professional life, is the subject of Chapter 6.

The writing of this book was both a painful and exhilarating experience. The pain came from examining and re-examining the individual and institutional sexism which academic women continue to endure. The exhilaration came from discovering the ability of these same women to prevail in the face of the massive and pervasive forces aligned against them. Although women have participated in American higher education for over 150 years, academic women are still pioneers, carving out a place for themselves in an unwelcoming, nonsupportive, and frequently hostile environment. Their energy and persistence in the continuing struggle is a source of inspiration.

1
Career Choices

And I remember having a lot of friends say, "Well, if I go to graduate school, I will not be a woman anymore and nobody will ever love me, but if I do go, I could have this great career." I mean, it never occurred to us that there wouldn't be jobs for us, regardless of whether it was a sort of acceptably female thing to do. And we in those years were supposed to get the sort of jobs that weren't careers so that we could wait around to be chosen by Prince Charming. What I am suggesting is that I always saw the academic world as not hostile to women. It was everything else that was hostile to our doing it.

—interview with a faculty woman

The first time I applied [to graduate school], they asked me, "What does a black woman like you want with a doctorate?" I went home with my feelings crushed. Then I came back another year and had a different experience. They were looking for black women. I met all the requirements; I got no breaks. But it was easier because they needed blacks for the program.

—interview with a faculty woman

If questioned, most people would probably say that the representation of women in all facets of academia has steadily increased since women first began to attend college in the mid-nineteenth century. Yet this has not been the case. In fact, according to Bernard's *Academic Women*, the best showing occurred in 1879-80, when women constituted 36.6 percent of academic personnel. From 1939 to 1962, the percentage steadily declined from 27.7 to 22 percent (Office of Education 1958-1963).

As one moved up the educational ladder, the proportion of women became smaller and smaller. For example, Bernard's data show that

5

in 1959-60, women made up 36.1 percent of the full-time college students, 35.3 percent of those receiving bachelor's degrees, 31.6 percent of those receiving master's degrees, and 10.9 percent of those receiving Ph.D.'s (Office of Education 1962).

Bernard wrestled with and never truly resolved the issue of whether the decline in academic women was due to direct discrimination or to a dwindling supply of women from which to choose. Part of her difficulty may have sprung from the way she defined discrimination. The key question for her was whether the criteria on which decisions regarding women were made were "functional" or "nonfunctional." Functional criteria, such as intelligence, training, and experience, are reasonable requirements for academic positions, and therefore are justifiable bases on which to discriminate between candidates for a job. However, the line between functional and nonfunctional criteria can be a hazy one, and that which seems like a functional criterion to some people may seem to others like an attempt to camouflage or justify prejudice. For example, according to Bernard, questions regarding women's commitment to their careers, as opposed to their families, served as a primary nonfunctional criterion on which their credentials were judged. Even if a woman were seriously considered, the assumption that she would either abandon or interrupt her career made hiring a man seem like a lower risk proposition (Bernard 1964).

Two criteria which are almost universally considered functional for academic positions are intelligence and academic achievement, on which Bernard found women to rank higher than men using objective measures. She cited a study showing that of all those receiving Ph.D.'s in 1958 and 1959, women scored higher than men in high school rank, intelligence tests, and general aptitude tests in mathematics and science (Harmon 1961). Other studies demonstrated the relationship between grade point average and plans to go to graduate school, showing that at each grade point level, a lower percentage of women planned to do graduate work. In fact, the percentage of women at each level corresponded to the percentage for men at the level below (Bernard 1964). This stands to reason, as there is a higher degree of selectivity at work for women, both imposed and presumably internal. Those who do aspire to graduate school must have stronger credentials to be taken seriously as candidates and to have confidence in their own ability to succeed.

In addition to strong academic credentials, Bernard found that women seemed to need more encouragement than men to pursue academic careers. One study of Ph.D. candidates cited by Bernard found that encouragement from college and high school teachers, friends, work associates, and spouses was more important for women than for men (Field 1961). Another showed women to be much more tentative, modest, and influenced by others in their academic career decisions (Eckert and Stecklein 1961). Perhaps because academia did not offer women the same built-in supports and access to networks and resources as it did men, they had to be deliberate in building their own individual support systems.

Bernard found that once having made the decision to enter academia, women chose certain fields more frequently than others. Women tended to be represented more heavily in fields such as English, journalism, foreign languages and literature, and the fine and applied arts, and less so in the physical sciences and mathematics (Snow 1959). In counting the proportion of female faculty members by field at 673 institutions in 1954-1955, home economics and library science were the only fields in which women comprised a majority; health professions and education were the only other fields in which they represented more than a third (Office of Education, 1958; and N.S.F. 1961). In general, women were more likely to be found in fields which were related to people rather than things.

These phenomena left Bernard with three possible explanations for the way in which women were distributed within academia. One was that women were the victims of discrimination, particularly within certain fields and institutions. The second was that women found fewer supports, both institutionally and within society at large, in the pursuit of particular careers. The third was that women make clear choices, based on true preferences for teaching, for example, or for people-oriented fields. While Bernard seemed most inclined towards the third explanation, she did not dismiss the importance of the other two, nor their direct and indirect impact on the choices women make.

Participation as Students

Today, women make up more than half of the undergraduate and graduate students participating in higher education. Although there are still fewer female graduate and professional students than there are male, and although there is a decrease in the percentage of women receiving degrees as one moves to more advanced degrees, the sharp decline of the early 1950s seems to have reversed itself (National Center for Educational Statistics 1982). In fact, women accounted for almost one third of all doctoral recipients in 1980-1981 (National Research Council 1982).

Clearly, women are more heavily represented in some fields than in others. Yet there seems to be a trend towards increasing participation in those fields in which women have been virtually invisible. For example, 99 of the 2,528 engineering Ph.D.'s awarded in 1981 went to women, in contrast to the total of 437 engineering Ph.D.'s awarded to women between 1920 and 1977 (Committee on the Education and Employment of Women in Science and Engineering 1979, 1983). Not only is the proportion of women relative to men increasing in these fields, but the proportion of women choosing them among all female doctoral recipients is increasing as well, although slightly (Table 1.1).

Credentials

As cited earlier, the existing research in Bernard's time showed that the women were stronger students than the men, as measured by such factors as high school rank, intelligence tests, and general aptitude tests. Most measures point to the same conclusions today.

Studies which compare scores on the Graduate Record Examination show male and female graduate students to be comparable, with men scoring higher on the quantitative tests and women higher on those measuring verbal ability (Solmon 1976). In studies of grade-point averages (GPA), female graduate students are generally shown as having done better academically as undergraduates than their male counterparts. In Feldman's study of 32,000 graduate students, for example, the median undergraduate GPA for women was B+,while the median for men was B (Feldman 1974).

Studies also show that a higher percentage of men go to graduate school than women, even among strong students. One study found that of those students with A to A+ averages, 70 percent of the men, but only 47 percent of the women, went on to graduate or professional school. Of those students with a B average, 45 percent of the men and 22 percent of the women continued their education. (Note that about the same proportion of men with B averages went to graduate school as did women with A/A+ averages [Baird 1976].)

Within individual fields, women tend to have higher GPAs as well. This is especially true in those fields in which women have been in the minority. Feldman's study showed that in the sciences, the percentage of female graduate students whose undergraduate GPA was B+ or better was significantly higher than the percentage of males. For example, in physiology the percentage of females with at least a B+ was 70.8, while the percentage of males was 42.9; in chemistry, the percentage of females was 62.9 while the percentage of males was 44.4 (Feldman 1974). All of these data suggest that women must be superior students even to consider going on to graduate programs; it could be inferred that they needed stronger credentials to be admitted.

While the higher GPAs of women have been dismissed as proof, not of academic achievement, but of greater compliance and co-operativeness, women also tend to rate higher than men in measures of intellectual ability. One study compared average I.Q.'s of men and women in graduate science departments ranked at different levels of quality according to Cartter ratings. Overall, and in the first, third and fourth levels of this four-tiered rating system, women's I.Q.'s were higher (Cole 1979).

In short, on virtually every objective measure, women graduate students continue to score, on average, higher or the same as men. In 1964, Bernard wrote:

> The test-type superiority of women doctoral recipients can be explained in part by the relatively greater selectivity operating among them. All along the line, the selective factors at work to produce academic women are more stringent than those at work to produce academic men.

The same phenomenon seems to be true today.

It is clear that women tend to cluster in certain fields (Table 1.2). The academic disciplines themselves also tend to be seen as either masculine or feminine. Three-hundred-fifty undergraduates in one study rated fields on their stereotyped imagery of masculinity/femininity. Engineering, agriculture, law, physics, dentistry, business, and architecture were seen as most masculine, while home economics, nursing, elementary education, library science, French, English, and social work were seen as most feminine (Feldman 1974). Further examination of these data shows a high correlation between perceived masculinity/femininity and the actual proportion of participation by women. As Saul Feldman recognized, this presents an interesting chicken and egg question.

We cannot establish causal ordering of the relationship between perceptions and enrollments; that is, we cannot state that certain fields are viewed as feminine and then women are encouraged to enter them or that women for some reason enter fields that are *then* defined as feminine. At this point there is reciprocity; because fields are viewed as feminine, women enter them, and because women are in them, they are viewed as feminine.

Closely related to the masculinity/femininity perception is the factor of prestige. Again, one is confronted with a chicken and egg question. Are women, for whatever reason, attracted to fields which are less prestigious, or are certain fields more prestigious because of their high degree of male participation? In a later work Bernard wrote:

Whatever men do, no matter what it is, has more prestige than what women do, even if it involves the same kinds of decisions, requires the same amount of education, and deals with equally serious responsibility. [Bernard 1971]

The prestige of a field is often judged by the degree of difficulty involved in becoming a member, and by the perceived glamor, as well as importance, of the work being produced. In Feldman's survey of graduate students, their responses to the items, "Exciting developments are taking place in my field," "My field is among the most respected academic disciplines," and "My field gets a good share of the best students," showed that fields such as medicine, biochemistry, physics, and mathematics rated the highest. Feldman wrote: "Prestigious fields appear to be where the action is, and that action is scientific research." Those same fields are also those with small percentages of women.

It is not surprising that in those fields where women comprise a minority, there is more prejudice against them. In a survey of 765 female graduate students at a large state university in 1975, the students reported the highest level of negative attitudes towards women from male faculty and from male and female graduate students in female minority departments, and the lowest level in female majority departments. This suggests that when people are unaccustomed to seeing women in a particular area, their attitudes may be influenced regarding the appropriateness of women's presence. There were no differences in the attitudes of female faculty in female minority, majority, or equalitarian departments (Holahan 1979). Similarly, Feldman found that in response to the item, "The female graduate students in my department are not as dedicated as the males," both graduate students (particularly men) and faculty were more likely to agree in fields that were male-dominated, or perceived as masculine. In the same fields, both male and female graduate students were more likely to respond affirmatively to "Professors in my department don't really take the female graduate students seriously."

Several of the faculty members interviewed for this study reported getting the message, either directly or indirectly, that certain fields were inappropriate for them as women. Some proceeded in defiance of those sentiments.

> I had always shown a talent for math and science. Consequently in high school, my teachers encouraged me to go to college to study either English or music, for which I had also shown some aptitude.

Others, despite their accomplishments, lived with a sense of undeveloped potential and lost opportunities.

> Health care in general was an interest. I was particularly adept at sciences. I think if I was encouraged, I would have gone to medical school, but that was not an encouragement. It was a big deal that I even wanted to go to college.

> I think in a perfect world, I would probably have been a scientist. I love what I do, I love to write. I went into kind of a women's profession and I just grew up assuming that there were things I couldn't do, but teaching English, you know. I think I might have done something different— not that I'm not happy, but I don't feel I chose to go into English. I just always assumed I would.

Women in Science

The sciences have always been the disciplines considered most masculine, both in the way in which they are conceived and in the overwhelming predominance of male participants, particularly at the upper levels. Women have been stereotypically perceived as not having the dedication, drive, rational objectivity, or creative intellectuality necessary to be successful scientists (Bernard 1964).

On one level, the paucity of women in the sciences is a matter of simple discrimination. On another, it is due to the nature of science itself as it is currently defined. In her essay, "Feminism and Science," Evelyn Fox Keller explained that the androcentric bias of the sciences goes beyond the choice and definition of problems to be investigated, or the research methodology or design, but rather to the very notion of objective inquiry, in which "objectivity is linked with autonomy and masculinity, and in turn, the goals of science with power and domination" (Keller 1983). This study will investigate further the implications of feminist scholarship at a later point. However, it must be noted that questions related to the participation rates of women in various fields go deeper than mere numbers, extending to the actual ethos of the field itself.

Despite such barriers, the percentage of women participating in the sciences has grown considerably over the past two decades, due to a large extent to affirmative action efforts. From 1972 to 1982, employment for women scientists and engineers increased by 200 percent, compared to 40 percent for men. While most women are employed in life and social sciences, the most rapid progress for women at the doctoral level is being made in engineering and computer sciences, where employment rose from a total of 100 in each field to over 700 from 1973 to 1981. Increases have also been rapid for minority women, with employment of both black and Asian female scientists and engineers growing by 400 percent over the 1972-82 decade (N.S.F. 1984). However, Table 1.3 shows the very small numbers of minority women within several scientific fields, rendering them virtually invisible within many.

Also discouraging are the individual accounts of women scientists who report system-supported prejudice against them from colleagues and superiors. In the extreme, one study shows a suicide rate for women chemists which is five times that of white American women as a whole, a figure which the authors suggest may be due in part to the male-dominated workplace (*Chemical and Engineer-*

ing News, 1984). Thus, while the numbers of women in the sciences are increasing, it is difficult to assess the extent to which their actual experience is changing, or to know how much potential is lost in those women who fall by the wayside, due to neglect, discouragement, sabotage, or outright exclusion. Vivian Gornick, in her work *Women in Science* (1983), strikes an optimistic note, however, in claiming that the women scientists of today show an exuberance and sense of entitlement unheard of in times past.

> The women doing science today are characterized by their variousness. Among them are women with the personalities of data-collectors, and others with the personalities of philosophers. They are truth-seekers and problem-solvers, abstractionists and competitors. Temperamentally, they fill the range from the visionary and the isolate to the compulsively sociable and the rogue maverick. The psyche and character of most contemporary women scientists has been wonderfully shaped by their newfound ability to be scientifically accomplished while at the same time retaining the full flavor of their individual being. Science now provides them with a culture of the working self within which one is both free and defined. Exactly as men have always been.
>
> At no moment before this have women scientists been free to be themselves; the exhibition of "temperament" and human variousness among them is a true event in scientific life; it signals a transformation; it means we have arrived at a point in the history of women in science where things may *look* as they have always looked (women half in, half out of science is still the greater truth), but enormous change is in process.

Gornick attributes this transformation to the contributions and accomplishments of the feminist movement rather than to the scientific professions themselves, and perhaps therein lies the key to true change in substance and style of the sciences, and to greater openness to a diversity of ideas and participants. One cannot expect systems which have been perpetuating themselves for decades to spontaneously reverse their course, particularly if it involves a perceived decrease in power for the original members. It has taken pressure—political, intellectual, legal, institutional, and financial—to ensure that women have been included to the extent that they have been. History seems to indicate that it will take continued pressure to extend those gains further.

Motivating Factors

Bernard found that academic women tended to come from a higher socioeconomic class background than academic men, and were more likely to have fathers who were in professional occupations (Gropper and Fitzpatrick 1959). Feldman's study of 12,000 graduate school men and women found that 43 percent of both came from homes in which the father had a white-collar or semiprofessional occupation. While the sex differential found by Bernard no longer exists, it can still be said that social class and family background are related to enrollment in graduate school for women. Perhaps the lower percentage of racial minorities, compared to whites, within the upper and professional classes has contributed to the smaller numbers of minority women in academic professions. Thus, racism has a double impact on the careers of minority women, by creating conditions which may limit their initial access to the professions, and by affecting their actual experiences once there.

Several of the faculty women interviewed for this study made reference to the influence of the professions of their parents.

> My father's a doctor, and I was the oldest child and the only girl, so it was always assumed that I would be a doctor.

> I came from an academic background. My mother was a secondary school teacher in classics and my father was a university professor and I'm sure that that was an influence, whether it was conscious or not.

Besides class background of the family, Bernard listed encouragement from family members as an important factor in women's decisions to go into academia. The potential influence of family is so great for women generally that research indicates that only or eldest female children, or those with no brothers, have a greater chance than other women for career success, as they are likely to be the focus of the family ambitions, and thus are encouraged in their achievements (Rivers et al. 1979). The women in this study did not talk about direct encouragement from family as much as they mentioned growing up in families in which their nontraditional interests and achievements were not discouraged.

> It's interesting because I have a sister who has a Ph.D. in chemistry and she and I've sat and talked about this. We're both in science, and this is not particularly common. And I think I was going to identify one big feature is a spirit that my father established in the household. I was never aware of role models and that women did this and men did that. All the way through high school—you know you can observe things like women are secretaries and certain things. So therefore, pursuing and thinking about pursuing a career that's more analytical or mathematical, like engineering, wasn't discouraged. It wasn't necessarily encouraged, but I know that I wasn't discouraged.

> I would say that my father was an influence. He always wanted to be an engineer, but grew up in the Depression, and couldn't go to college and for a while I thought I wanted to be an engineer too, but as I got through college, I realized that it was what he wanted to do.

While most of the faculty women who talked about their families as influences cited their fathers, a few mentioned their mothers.

> My mother had been a librarian. My father absolutely did not let her work when she got married, and she never went back to it at all. But she enjoyed it very much and she spoke of it with such enthusiasm and I think I caught it from her. She always had the feeling, even back then, that women had just as much right as anybody else to do that, and to have important careers and to enjoy what they were doing. So I think I kind of picked it up, not because she made speeches to me about it, but because her attitude was so enthusiastic about the work that she had done.

As suggested by Bernard, several of the women described their careers as if they had fallen into them, rather than having made a deliberate decision to pursue one area or another. In some cases, this was influenced by the type or location of their husbands' career; in others, by strong encouragement from faculty members.

> Well, I think I fell into an academic career. I never really thought very much about it. When I was in my senior year of college, I knew I was getting married. I was engaged; my husband wanted to go to law school. I decided I wanted to go to graduate school. That was my goal—to go to graduate school—I wasn't thinking beyond to career. And I decided to go to graduate school in economics rather than math because I liked economics better.

> I really didn't know what to do with myself and the sociology major, and I was kind of toying with law school, which is what I understand a lot of people who don't know that they want to do, do, at which point I started to, quite honestly, get flattered by some of my sociology professors, who suggested that I go to graduate school in sociology for the Ph.D., and they gave me a lot of positive reinforcement about one particular area of sociology, where the 'Head Honcho' of the area was teaching at U._____. So their recommendations and their pushing, and I guess my lack of knowing what it was that I wanted to do—I went to U._____ and enrolled in the Ph.D. program, which I liked.

> At the same time I had all along been taking oddball graduate courses. I had no intention of getting a degree, but at that point, Dr. T decided that I was married to a faculty member, and that meant I was going to be around a university, probably one university or another, for the rest of my life, and if I wanted to work in a university you need what is known as a union card. I then registered for a degree, while I was working.

In some cases, this encouragement was accompanied by an actual opportunity to teach.

> One of my professors said, "Instead of that [student teaching in a junior high school], why don't you teach one of my undergraduate classes in composition?" . . . and I was anxious to try it. I was much more interested in English

and writing than I was in junior high school. I did that, and then I began to get a sense that maybe I should be a college teacher.

. . . Some boredom, some looking for other things, probably some faculty seeing that I had some potential. After I graduated there was a faculty member who had to take a leave of absence due to illness. They asked me if I would teach on a part-time basis that semester and then I stayed. . . . So obviously, I guess they thought I had something going for me.

It makes sense that women would need encouragement before embarking on an academic career. If young women are not accustomed to seeing female role models in academia, then they may not even consider the possibility that they themselves have the ability and the perseverance to succeed. Being singled out for recognition of their talents and for support of their efforts might have been just the extra push that was needed to expand the scope of their career options. Women in present-day American society were generally not raised with the notion that they could grow up to choose from all available careers. Thus, while these women were perhaps not "bound and determined" from an early age to become faculty members, that does not mean that their commitment to their fields, once chosen, was less real than for their male counterparts, as is often accused. Given the obstacles women face, this commitment may indeed have to be a stronger one for them to persevere.

There were a few motivating factors mentioned by the faculty women interviewed for this study that seemed contrary to Bernard's findings. She wrote, for example, that women tend to have a lower competitive drive than men, either by choice, by nature, or due to the relatively smaller rewards they receive. Again, this seems unlikely in light of the greater effort women must expend to maintain equal footing with their graduate student or faculty peers, having started at a disadvantage given the attitudes and actions they face. If faculty women truly lacked the drive to succeed, then it is more likely that they would have chosen less competitive careers or would have dropped out along the way. Women's lower status than men's on measures of rank and salary should not be seen as the result of lower competitiveness; rather, their very presence in the academy should be seen as proof of their ability and willingness to strive against high odds and strong resistance. Several of the women listed their strong drive to be the best as important to them in their pursuit of the doctorate.

> I liked biology a lot and I'd always been self-motivated . . . so I'd always been different from my girlfriends, and my boyfriends, even. I'd always been kind of driven.

> . . . a need to be successful, I guess, and I guess I was always taught to do the best I possibly could, and I could do better in intellectual things than other things.

> And when I got to graduate school, the normal compulsion to excel—I didn't think so much about a career that was motivating everybody else. It was just being competitive and trying to outdo everybody else, whatever the goals were.

One faculty member mentioned money as an important factor in her decision to switch her field.

> That went on for two years until I decided not to go on to get the Ph.D. because there was a glut of sociologists . . . but the salaries of sociology professors were absolutely horrendously low. Money's not my prime motivating factor—but it's up there.

As reported earlier in this chapter, Bernard cited research that stated that women were less likely to choose academic careers due to factors directly associated with the job itself, but rather due to external factors, such as encouragement from others. Yet several of the women mentioned their enthusiasm for and interest in their disciplines and their general love of learning as important reasons for continuing with their educations. Both women quoted below seem to have almost been caught by surprise that their delight in learning could translate into a career.

> I found myself in my third year of graduate school finishing a Ph.D., and then thinking about what I was going to do—at that point being very concerned about a career, having accomplished all this, to be sure I was going to be able to use it. But I wasn't that much directed towards

that goal—it was the sheer pleasure of the experience of being in graduate school and undergraduate school that motivated me.

So it's really true that I did fall into it, in a way. I mean, I cannot claim to have been always bound and determined to have a career. Really, the excitement that I find in working with social statistics pushed me into wanting to continue, and I think, even if we hadn't worked out a system whereby I could continue working, I would have done that on my own.

Thus, for the women interviewed in this study, there were a number of different reasons for pursuing academic careers. It seems, as Bernard suggested, that encouragement from family and professors, or at least the absence of active discouragement, was important in the motivation of faculty women. Other factors included a drive to be the best, money, and a passion for the subject matter itself. Some felt a sense of being "mislocated," in that their true talents and interests might have been in other areas had they been able to develop freely. It seems that the simple pursuit of an academic career for the benefits of the career itself was not a strong motivator, perhaps because of all the attendant difficulties of academic careers for women.

Jean Baker Miller wrote that the greater ability of women, compared to men, to admit feelings of vulnerability should be seen as a strength rather than a weakness, because these feelings are common to all and should be more freely expressed (Miller 1976). However, the fact that women seem to need more support and encouragement than men has been used by some as evidence that women lack the toughness and confidence to excel in academia, as well as other professions. What is lacking in that assumption is recognition of the implicit support which men receive both from individuals and through the natural functioning of the institutional climate. Where men have institutional and family supports, women must go about creating their own. (It is interesting to note that both in 1964 and today, academic men were far more likely to be married than academic women, and that having a spouse was more likely to be associated with career success for men than for women.) Perhaps it is not that women need more encouragement, per se, but rather that they seek to equalize their situation with that of men. Likewise, the support which men receive may be invisible to the observer because it is so woven into the fabric of everyday academic life. Women may indeed need more deliberate efforts on their behalf, but not necessarily greater ones.

This is not only true of women's decisions to embark on academic careers, but of their choice of fields as well. There is ongoing debate as to whether women are channeled into certain areas, or whether their interests and abilities are indeed different from men's. Historically and currently, women are more likely to be found in "people-oriented" than "things-oriented" fields. One may ask whether this is due to women's granting greater value than men to relationships, as suggested by Carol Gilligan's work (Gilligan 1982). However, it may be premature to answer this question, given the levels of discrimination through which women must work in making their choice of career and field.

First, those choices may be limited, not necessarily by law, but by the boundaries of traditional practices and attitudes. Thus, a women may face a restricted horizon of options. A woman who is talented in science and enjoys working with people, for example, may choose nursing rather than a career in medicine or dentistry. A woman who enjoys organization and management may choose home economics or library science, rather than business administration. Also, women may be motivated by different factors than men in making career choices, and may be less motivated by money and status in their decision-making. These choices may indeed reflect preferences; they may also be constrained by stereotyped imagery of appropriate masculine or feminine interests and abilities.

This restricted range of options may be limited by the inability of individuals to even see beyond traditional practices and patterns, or it may be the result of a realistic appraisal of the compounded difficulties women face when they veer off their conventional paths. A woman may not even consider pursuing a career as a research scientist, knowing the barriers she would encounter, so she may decide to channel her talents into training future scientists. Another may see the difficulty of combining a career in engineering with raising a family, so she may pursue a career in math education instead. This is not to suggest that these choices are simply defaults, or that women have opted out of the competition and therefore are to blame for their lower participation rates, but rather that women may tailor their aspirations to a realistic assessment of their chances for success.

Equally interesting is the impact women may have on various fields as they enter them in greater numbers. For example, will there be upward and downward shifts in prestige for different fields as the male/female ratio within them becomes more balanced? Will the perceived masculinity or femininity of fields change as the participation rates change? More important, to what extent will the central issues and questions within fields shift as women enter them, bringing their own interests, experiences, and perspectives? Further, will women shake the very core of intellectual inquiry, raising questions about the values and functions of scholarship, and about the appropriate role of the scholar herself? These same questions are asked whenever women enter a predominantly male arena, such as business, law, or government.

Perhaps initially, greater numbers of women will merely signify greater access and opportunity within the system. The inclusion of more women does not necessarily mean a concomitant growth in commitment to feminist ideals and principles. However, as participation rates increase and as more women rise within the academic hierarchy, it seems likely that they will have an impact on the essence and foundations of scholarship for both men and women. Already, that appears to be the case, even if only in rudimentary form.

Thus perhaps there is some validity to the fears of some that the injection of greater numbers of women will alter the academy in both style and substance. However, 'different' does not necessarily signify a diminished quality or vigor; rather, it is likely to mean a new vitality, as previously closed systems are swept open to include new participants and new perspectives. It would not be sufficient for higher education simply to increase the numbers of women and minorities within the system if that system continues to be male-dominated in its policies, practices, epistemologies, values, methodologies, and structures.

One of the ways in which this male-centered system has been perpetuated has been through the channeling of women away from the higher reaches of academic achievement, and into certain fields. This task has not been accomplished solely by academic institutions, but in combination with prejudice, discrimination, and lack of support within general societal institutions as well. All together, this creates a situation in which women must struggle harder than men to gain a foothold on the academic ladder, and must fashion their own individual combination of support, encouragement, and self-confidence to achieve success. They must be deliberate in these efforts to achieve parity with men, for whom these things are implicit within the entire academic system. With the inspiration of the pioneers such as Barbara McClintock, Margaret Mead, and countless others whose talents went underutilized and unrecognized, with the strength of the growing numbers of women within all fields, and with the power of the law and the clout of women's organizations, women are struggling to fully pursue their interests and develop their talents for the first time in the history of American higher education.

TABLE 1.1
Percentage of Women among Doctoral Degree Recipients and Percentage of Women Doctoral Recipients by Discipline, 1971 and 1977.

	1971 % of Total Ph.D's Awarded Women	% of Total Women Ph.D Recipients	1977 % of Total Ph.D's Awarded Women	% of Total Women Ph.D Recipients	% Gain Among Women Ph.D. Recipients
All Disciplines	14.3	100.0	24.3	100.0	—
Agriculture and Natural Resources	2.9	.68	6.9	.76	.08
Arch. & Envir. Design	8.3	.07	15.1	.14	.14
Area Studies	17.4	.56	32.0	.61	.05
Biological Science	16.3	12.94	21.4	9.01	−3.93
Business and Management	2.8	.49	6.3	.68	.19
Communications	13.1	.41	24.0	.51	.10
Computer and Information	2.3	.06	8.8	.24	.18
Education	21.3	29.54	34.8	32.27	4.73
Engineering	.6	.48	2.8	.90	.52
Fine and Applied Arts	22.2	3.00	32.5	2.66	−.34
Foreign Languages	38.0	6.46	51.5	4.79	−1.67
Health Professions	16.5	1.67	32.0	2.13	.46
Home Economics	61.0	1.63	77.0	1.53	−.10
Law	0.0	0.00	13.3	.10	.10
Letters	23.5	12.36	38.2	10.41	−1.95
Library Science	28.2	.24	53.3	.49	.25
Mathematics	7.8	2.04	13.2	1.34	−.70
Physical Sciences	5.6	5.35	9.6	3.97	−1.38
Psychology	24.0	9.31	35.9	12.27	2.96
Public Affairs and Services	24.2	.94	32.8	1.36	.42
Social Sciences	13.9	11.08	22.1	10.35	−.73
Theology	1.9	.13	2.8	.39	.26
Interdisciplinary Studies	15.4	.31	30.6	1.15	.84

SOURCE: Mary L. Spencer and Eva Bradford, "Status and Needs of Women Scholars," in *Handbook for Women Scholars*, eds. Mary L. Spencer, Monika Kehoe, and Karen Speece (San Francisco: Americas Behavioral Research Corporation, 1982), p. 8.

TABLE 1.2
Recipients of Doctorates, by Field and Sex, 1981-82.

Field	Men	Women
Arts and Humanities	57.6%	42.4%
Computer Sciences	90.9%	9.1%
Education	51.2%	48.8%
Engineering	95.3%	4.7%
Life Sciences	72.3%	27.7%
Mathematics	86.7%	13.3%
Physical Sciences	86.3%	13.7%
Social Sciences	63.3%	36.7%
All Fields	67.6%	32.4%

SOURCE: *Survey of Earned Doctorates*, National Research Council, cited in "A Profile of 1981-82 Recipients of Doctorates," *Chronicle of Higher Education*, 7 September 1983, p. 14. Copyright 1986 by the *Chronicle of Higher Education*. Reprinted with Permission.

TABLE 1.3
Women Doctoral Scientists and Engineers by Field and Race, 1981

Field	Total[1]	Total population			
		White	Black	Asian	Native American
Total S/E	45,700	40,700	1,100	3,100	300
Total scientists	45,000	40,000	1,100	3,000	300
Physical scientists	4,400	3,500	(2)	700	(2)
Chemists	3,700	2,900	(2)	600	(2)
Physicists/astronomers	700	600	(2)	100	(2)
Mathematical scientists	1,500	1,200	(2)	200	(2)
Mathematicians	1,200	1,000	(2)	100	(2)
Statisticians	300	200	(2)	100	(2)
Computer specialists	700	600	(2)	100	(2)
Environmental scientists	900	800	(2)	100	(2)
Earth scientists	600	600	(2)	(2)	(2)
Oceanographers	200	200	(2)	(2)	(2)
Atmospheric scientists	100	100	(2)	(2)	(2)
Life scientists	15,200	13,300	300	1,400	100
Biological scientists	10,600	9,300	200	900	100
Agricultural scientists	500	400	(2)	100	(2)
Medical scientists	4,000	3,600	100	300	(2)
Psychologists	12,800	11,900	400	300	100
Social scientists	9,500	8,700	300	300	(2)
Economists	1,300	1,200	(2)	100	(2)
Sociologists/anthropologists	3,300	3,000	100	100	(2)
Other social scientists	5,000	4,500	200	200	(2)
Engineers	800	600	(2)	100	(2)

[1]Includes racial categories listed as well as Other and No report.
[2]Too few cases to estimate.
Note: Detail may not add to totals because of rounding.
SOURCE: National Science Foundation, Characteristics of Doctoral Scientists and Engineers in the United States: 1981 (NSF 82-332) and unpublished data, cited in *Women and Minorities in Science and Engineering* (Washington: National Science Foundation, 1984), pp. 71–72.

2
Measures of Formal Status

The universities, especially their graduate and professional schools, have become pacesetters in the promotion of meritocratic values. In Talcott Parson's terms, they are "universalistic," ignoring "particularistic" and personal qualities in their students and professors. This means that they choose professors almost entirely on the basis of their "output" and professional reputation . . . The claims of localism, sectarianism, ethnic prejudice and preference, class background, age, sex, and even occupational plans are largely ignored.

> —*Christopher Jencks and David Riesman (1968)*

The most important thing for you to know is this: They will try to persuade you that you are being denied tenure (or promotion, or reappointment) because of your deficiencies. The argument most certain to take you in is the one that speaks to your self-doubt, so they will tell you that your publications are mediocre, your teaching weak. Don't believe it.

> —*Marcia Lieberman (1981)*

Within academia, there is little obvious difference among the types of activities in which faculty members at different ranks are expected to engage. Regardless of seniority, ability, or performance, faculty members traditionally devote their efforts, to a greater or lesser extent, within three general categories: teaching, research, and community service. In this respect, academics are different from other occupations, in which people at different status levels perform very different functions.

The homogeneity ends there, however. For one thing, there is a clear understanding that certain institutions are of better quality and hold more prestige than others (although the determination of those formal or informal rankings may be hotly debated). Also, within institutions there are clear status distinctions between the tenured and nontenured, part-time and full-time, tenure-track and adjunct, and among the various rank and salary levels. While individuals may be performing similar or identical functions, they may be worlds apart in status within their institution, field, or profession.

All determinations of status within higher education are based on two assumptions: 1) that the academy is a meritocracy, and 2) that the professoriate is a profession. Particularly now that shrinking enrollments and budgets are forcing institutions to scrutinize these decisions more closely, good performance alone is not considered sufficient for salary increases, promotion, or tenure. Nothing less than excellence is sought, albeit in poorly defined measures that are usually difficult to assess. Almost by definition, the process is a highly subjective one. Logan Wilson (1979) writes:

> The hierarchy of prestige in academic fields, as in all others, is never identical with merit. Judgment of merit, in turn, as well as the capacity to assess it, differ according to the level and segment of the hierarchy rendering the verdict. The competitive system and whatever scale of values academics may choose or have forced upon them determine their ideology of success.

While the system employs the rhetoric of merit, its determination is far from objective. Even if there were agreement on the most important criteria, for example, agreement on means of assessment and actual performance would be difficult to reach. The process which is constructed to sort out the mediocre and the merely good at each level may be sorting factors other than merit, as well. Some of these may include political or social affiliations, intellectual perspective, or perceived congeniality.

Further complicating the issue of status are the mechanisms through which the decisions are reached. Like other professional groups, the professoriate asserts that only those within the profession are able to make judgments about its members' work. What is more, faculty members often resist judgments made outside of a given discipline, or even subspecialty, pointing out that a physicist may indeed have difficulty judging the work of a Slavist, and vice versa. Often, opinions from within disciplines, but outside the institution, are sought.

Autonomy and self-governance are the hallmarks of the academic profession. As Logan Wilson (1979) writes: "By and large, theirs is the main say in the selection, retention or termination, and promotion of colleagues; few employees in other organizations have such powers." While there is certainly value in the high degree of autonomy permitted in academic decision-making, there are drawbacks as well. Decisions are highly subjective, with politics and personalities almost necessarily coloring decisions on merit. Difference—by sex, by race, by intellectual orientation—can be seen by the majority as "less-than-excellence." Certainly there is a high degree of homogeneity among those who have survived the system to reach its highest levels.

Representation of Women Faculty

Since the 1960s, there has been dramatic change in the numbers of women within the student ranks (see Chapter 1). In 1981, women made up more than half of the undergraduate and graduate students (although less than one quarter of the professional students) and received 31.5 percent of all doctorates (National Center for Educational Statistics 1982; and N.R.C. 1982). Between 1970 and 1980, there was a 27 percent increase in the number of bachelor's degrees earned by women, an 800 percent increase in first professional degrees, a 63 percent in master's degrees, and a 100 percent increase in doctorates (*Chronicle of Higher Education* 23 June 1982).

Yet despite this growth in the pool of qualified women, there has not been much change over the past two decades in the overall representation of women within the faculty ranks. Women now hold 27.5 percent of all faculty positions (*Chronicle of Higher Education* 10 Sept. 1986). The picture is even bleaker for minority women, who represented 3 percent of all full-time faculty in 1976, with black women accounting for 2 percent, Asian women .4 percent, Hispanic women .4 percent, and Native American women less than .1 percent (Vetter and Babco 1978). However, women have been making up a larger percentage of those currently being hired to faculty positions. For example, in universities, 22.4 percent of the newly hired in 1980 were women, as compared to 14.7 percent in 1972; in four-year colleges, the figure was 28 percent compared to 19. Selective institutions (those with student SATs of 1160 or higher) hired one quarter of the total number of faculty women hired between 1975 and 1980 (Astin and Snyder 1982). This is especially significant in light of the shrinking academic job market of the past decade.

The increase in the hiring of women has been particularly sharp in areas where women have been in the minority. Between 1973 and 1977, in the top 25 institutions, the percentage of women faculty increased by 62 percent in the category of scientific disciplines which included mathematics, physics/astronomy, chemistry, earth sciences, and engineering. It increased by 41.3 percent in life sciences, and by 69.4 percent in psychology and the social sciences (N.R.C. 1979).

Women have always played a larger role than their numbers on the faculty may indicate. A disproportionately large number of women have always served in part-time positions, or as lecturers or instructors, off the tenure track and outside of the possibility of promotion. Jessie Bernard commented that these women "constitute an elastic labor pool, hired and furloughed as needed." As Bernard saw it, these women were likely to be the wives of academic men, with different aspirations, role conceptions and self-definitions than the professional academician. There are many today who would dispute whether the woman in a part-time or nontenure track position was there by choice. One study of 588 institutions in 1976 showed that women held 38 percent of the part-time positions but only 25 percent of the full-time positions. The same study showed women holding 44 percent of the full-time nontenure track positions, but only 18 percent of the full, associate or assistant professorships (Howard 1978). Similarly, of those Ph.D.'s in science in 1975 who wanted full-time work, more women than men were employed part-time, employed in nonscience jobs because positions in science were not available, or unemployed altogether (Maxfield et al. 1976). Women continue to hold a higher share of those positions which are part-time, nontenure track, or outside of their primary sphere of interest. The overall employment picture, compounded by a generally tighter academic job market, remains the same as it was in 1964.

A key index of academic status is the institution with which one is affiliated. Although the exact ranking of different institutions may be hotly debated, there is no question that certain individual and categories of institutions are considered more prestigious than others. In Bernard's time, women were more likely to be found in lower status institutions, such as teacher-training and two-year colleges, and less likely to be at prestigious research-oriented universities (Office of Education 1958). Table 2.1 shows the same pattern to exist today, with women clustered in two-year and teaching-oriented institutions rather than research-oriented ones. Two striking examples are Harvard University, with only 21 tenured faculty women among the 355 tenured faculty in 1984 (Sanger 1985), and Yale University, with 17 women out of 320 tenured faculty in 1985 (*Chronicle of Higher Education* 8 May 1985). Women faculty are also more likely to be found at women's colleges than at co-ed ones, and at smaller institutions than larger ones.

Salary

In *Academic Women*, Jessie Bernard pointed out the discrepancies between men and women in both rank and salary. She reported that women consistently held inferior academic rank, even when qualifications, such as holding a doctorate or productivity, were held constant. Bernard also found that type of institution and field had a relationship to the proportion of women in each rank. Of course, it makes sense that in those fields and institutions in which women were most heavily represented that they should be more heavily represented in the higher ranks. However, even in those fields and institutions, their proportion in those ranks did not equal their overall proportion. Women tended to be clustered at the lower end of the ladder, particularly in the heavily male-dominated disciplines (Parrish 1962).

Bernard reported salary discrepancies between men and women. In 1959-60, the median salary of male professors was $9,179, while the median salary for female professors was $7,899, making a 16.2 percent difference of $1,280. For instructors, the difference was $306, or 6.3 percent ($5,161 for men, $4,855 for women). The difference for all ranks combined was $1,041 or 17.7 percent ($6,906 for men, $5,865 for women) (N.E.A. 1960). In other words, the gap widened as one moved up the ladder.

Current research shows that the salary gap still exists, and that it continues to widen as one moves up the ladder. In 1982-83, female assistant and associate professors earned 94 percent of that earned by males, and female professors made 90 percent of male's salaries.

Overall, women's salaries were 83 percent of male's salaries (National Center for Education Statistics 1984).

Other studies also show that the longer women have been employed, the smaller their salary is likely to be in relation to men. A 1977 study of science doctorates showed that in the social sciences there was a 2.8 percent salary difference between male and female assistant professors, but a 13.1 percent difference at the full professor level. In chemistry, the gap widened from 7 percent to 28.3 percent; in medical science, from 5.5 percent to 17.2 percent (N.R.C 1979). Another study showed that at the beginning of their careers, women in anthropology were at a 8.5 percent disadvantage relative to men; after 30 years, they were at a 28 percent disadvantage. In mathematics, the disadvantage grew from 6.2 percent to 29.1 percent; in physics, from 9 percent to 22 percent (Johnson and Stafford 1979).

While there have recently been efforts to equalize salaries by giving women equal or greater salary increases, the gap still remains. Table 2.2 shows the average salaries for men and women faculty in 1983-84, by institutional type and field. In the humanities, for example, where women have received 7.7 percent salary increases, compared to 6 percent for men, their average salaries are still almost $4500 less. At public institutions, with a .5 percent larger increase, women's salaries still lag $5000 behind.

These data demonstrate the cumulative effects of discrimination, as discrimination against women early in their careers is perpetuated and magnified as their careers progress. The percentage of increase for men and women at different ranks for different institutional types is fairly similar, with men having a small advantage in most categories (A.A.U.P. 1982). However, because salary increases begin from a base salary, the gap widens as a lower starting salary is compounded by lower annual increments.

To address the claim that men and women are paid differently because their accomplishments are different, Astin and Bayer compared actual and predicted salaries for single and married women with those of men. The predicted mean salary was derived from a regression analysis, based on factors that were significant predictors of men's salaries, such as highest degree obtained, publication record, field, and type of institution. If men and women were compensated equally for their accomplishments, then the actual salary for women should have equalled the predicted one. However, in 1972, the difference between actual and predicted salary for married women was $1,522 and for single women was $1,895 (Astin and

Bayer 1979). Replicating the same methodology in 1980, the actual salary for single women was $1,080 higher than the predicted one, while the actual salary for married women still lagged $421 behind predicted (Astin and Snyder 1982). The evidence shows that women may be more likely today than in the past to receive equal compensation for equal performance.

Rank

However, Astin's 1980 findings are not as encouraging for rank. Using the same regression analysis model, comparing actual and predicted rank, women's rank is one-fourth of a step lower than predicted. Her 1972 study showed the predicted rank for women to be one-tenth of a step above the actual rank. It seems that women have lost some ground with respect to rank.

Many studies have cited the tendency for women to be clustered at the lower end of the academic ladder. As Table 2.3 shows, this is even more likely to be true in prestigious institutions, and it is even more true today than it was twenty-five years ago.

In looking at the data presented in Table 2.3, one can see that the overall share of women in faculty jobs in 1981-82 (24.3 percent) has not changed dramatically from the proportion, cited by Bernard, of women in a survey of 98 institutions in 1958-59 (19.1 percent). The two numbers might have been even closer had she included two-year institutions. Even so, the proportion of women at full professor rank is virtually identical, twenty-three years later (9.5 percent in 1958-59; 9.7 percent in 1981-82). The greatest growth has occurred at the associate rank (from 8.0 percent to 20.6 percent), assistant rank (20.8 percent to 35.1 percent) and instructor rank (30.7 percent to 53.3 percent) (Ward 1960; and A.A.U.P. 1982).

The significantly greater number of women at lower ranks has frequently led to the claim of a "revolving door" for women—that they are hired to fill short-term assistant professorships, to fulfill affirmative action requirements, but are not seriously considered for tenure or promotion. In the sciences, for example, women account for *all* of the net growth between 1973 and 1977 in science faculty at the assistant professor rank in the top universities, and nearly half of the increase in all other institutions. But at the full-professor rank during the same time period, they are responsible for only 19 percent of the net growth at the top institutions and six percent in the other institutions (Committee 1979).

Others have claimed that women have not entered various fields in great numbers, whether by choice or opportunity, until relatively recently, and that it will take more time for them to progress through the system. For example, a study of female business faculty showed that those who joined the faculty ranks after 1970 were better prepared and qualified than those who had been there longer. While women held lower ranks overall, when looking at only those faculty members with doctorates, male/female differences in rank disappeared (Robertson, 1979). Those entering the business faculty more recently were better able to compete on equal terms with men, and were successfully doing so.

Tenure

However, Astin showed that overall, even as recently as 1980, women were not advancing at the same rate as men. She found an increase of 17.7 percentage points in the proportion of men with tenure, from 68.5 percent of all male faculty in 1972 to 86.2 percent in 1980. For women, the proportion with tenure only increased by 13.4 percentage points from 54.6 percent of all female faculty to 68 percent (Astin and Snyder 1981).

One study of the percentages of female faculty members with tenure by institutional type showed that the greatest rate of increase from 1973 to 1976 was 1 percent (at schools of 1,000 to 5,000) while most categories had an increase of between .1 and .5 percent (Howard 1978).

As with salary and rank, there are also differences in tenure rates for different academic disciplines. Table 2.4 shows the number and percent of tenured male and female associate professors of science with Ph.D.'s in 1975 and 1977. Except in earth sciences and agricultural science, where the number of women is minuscule, the percentage of men with tenure is higher than the percentage of women. In 1981-82, 70 percent of all male faculty had tenure, compared to 50 percent of female faculty (National Center for Education Statistics 1978-81).

On all measures of formal status, women lag behind men. In fact, it is difficult to separate one factor from another, as women's standing in one has an impact on their standing in the others. For example, one researcher speculated that salary discrimination may be further compounded by slower promotion rates for women, because omitting rank as an exploratory variable raised the salary differential by sex from 19 to 35 percent, to 56 to 68 percent (Hoffman 1976). Similarly, an institution may not promote a woman to the associate professor rank if it has reservations about granting her a lifelong commitment of tenure. Women as a group may have a lower average salary than men because they tend to be located at those institutions which pay their faculty less. It is difficult to assess which factor is the driving force in the lower status of women, and to understand the mechanisms by which those forces work.

Explanations for the Differential

There are some who feel that the differential is not caused by discrimination, but rather by the market's reaction to choices made by women about their careers. Using a 'human capital accumulation' model, Johnson and Stafford (1974) attribute the gap to women's tendency to devote fewer hours to work, to spend less time in training, and to interrupt their careers for child-bearing. According to their theory, over the course of their careers, as women continue to be less involved, the salary differential grows.

There is not much support in the literature, however, for this model. Stephan Farber, in an examination of 12,000 doctoral scientists employed in colleges and universities, found that only the youngest group of women received smaller rates of salary than men. After six years of full employment, they received the same salary increases, although their actual salaries never caught up. He found the same trend to be true for rank, with the youngest age cohort of females receiving fewer rank promotions. He concluded that a woman will receive the same increases and promotions as a man "only if she shows that she is a consistent labor force participant" (Farber 1977). Even uninterrupted participation was not enough to offset the initial negative effect of being female. Rather than institutions responding to women's careers actually being interrupted for childrearing, as Johnson and Strafford claimed, they seemed to reward women based on the assumption that they would, whether or not this turned out to be true. Farber stated, "Apparently, females have to 'prove' their professional interest before receiving rank and salary increases."

Another study directly disputed the assumption that women interrupt their careers for childrearing, in showing that of 2,000 women who received their doctorates in 1957-1958, 79 percent had not interrupted their careers seven to eight years after receiving their Ph.D.'s. Of those that had, the median interruption was fourteen months (Astin 1969). Also, in looking at data on 212 female academic economists in 1974, only nine percent had had a gap of six months or more since receiving their Ph.D.'s. For women over 35, only 12 percent had a gap of six months or more (Stroeber and Quester 1977).

Bernard gave what she called 'status channel inconsistency' as an important explanation for the gap between women and men. There are several channels for status mobility for faculty within academia in general, and within specific institutions, although the relative importance of the different channels may or may not be clearly articulated or understood. Someone may achieve a high degree of status within one channel without achieving a high degree of institutional status. Women tended to be high achievers in channels which tended to not be highly valued, such as teaching or working with students, rather than research.

There is considerable evidence for the status channel inconsistency described by Jessie Bernard. Women choose or reject, or are encouraged towards or excluded from, certain aspects of the professorial role. One tenured faculty member observed:

What I hope other women don't go through is—all through my time in the academic world, I have seen women go under or become very unhappy because of being pressured to be nice . . . I think the great trap of young women today is that there is a sort of subtle pressure to be compliant, to not assert themselves intellectually, to spend 80 million times more time with students than the men do, to be motherly and nurturing, to be on a million committees, not to be a power within the university but to just do the drudgery that has to be done, to be compliant in every way. And then they don't get tenure and they fail. They don't say no to these demands, and these are demands that are much more put on women.

Within many institutions, particularly those with high prestige, scholarly productivity is the primary channel for success. And most of the research shows that women are not as productive as men.

In a 1972 survey of more than 10,000 faculty members from 301 institutions, Astin found that more than one third of the men, but less than one fifth of the women, spent more than eight hours a week in scholarly research and writing. Over one third of the men had published at least five articles and 7 percent at least one book (Astin and Bayer). In 1980, these publication proportions remained unchanged (Astin and Snyder). Another study, controlling factors such as marital status, number of children, time since Ph.D., teaching undergraduates, and hours in the classroom, found that women who responded to a Carnegie-American Council on Education survey had published 20 percent fewer articles than the men (Hamovitch and Morganstern 1977).

However, women whose productivity is equal to that of men find that their rewards are smaller. Cole found that quantity and quality of scientific output are not as strongly correlated with academic rank for female scientists as for males (Cole 1979). If institutions would pay the average female the average salary of a comparable male, then she would receive a bonus comparable to what she would receive for publishing ten books, or eleven to twenty articles (Tuckman 1979).

One possible reason for this discrepancy in rewards is that the work of women does not seem to be valued as highly as men's. First, women's work tends generally to be judged less favorably than men's. Second, when women do research on topics of particular interest to them, particularly from a feminist perspective, it may be automatically dismissed as minor or self-serving work by mainstream academics. This study will address both these phenomena in more depth at a later point.

There is still validity, then, to Bernard's contention that some of the status differences for women stem from their lack of success in some of the more institutionally valued status channels. One could argue whether this status channel inconsistency was a result of choice, ability, lack of opportunity, or exclusion. By the same token, it also seems that even when women do all the "right" things, they are rewarded less than men. In study after study, when measures such as scholarly productivity, administrative experiences, degree held, and years of experience are held constant, there is still a gap between women and men.

Another possible explanation for the differential offered by Bernard and others was that women are simply not as competitive as men. Whether by choice or by nature, they did not seem to be as concerned with striving for the highest status levels.

One study, however, offers evidence that this is not the case. In response to a survey of a random sample of 444 male and female assistant professors at all land grant universities, 79 percent of the females and 84 percent of the males indicated that they had discussed salary when first interviewed for their current position. Thirty-two percent of the females and 37 percent of the males attempted to negotiate a higher salary, and 61 percent of the women and 64 percent of the men were successful in doing so. Once working, 32 percent of the women and 35 percent of the men asked for raises, with 96 percent of the men and 99 percent of the women saying they would not resign if they did not receive them (DeReimer et al. 1982). While there are some small differences between the two, men and women were quite similar in their needs and their willingness to act on them, indicating that women may not be less motivated by needs for formal status, less concerned with material rewards, or less willing and able to be assertive on their own behalf.

If, then, women seem to want and strive for the same levels of formal status, and if they perform well in the "important" status channels, why do they continue to lag behind men? Spencer and Bradford (1982) list the following nine phenomena that are cited frequently by academic women as institutional barriers to their progress:

1) Absence of objective hiring and promotion criteria;
2) Use of informal, shifting hiring and promotion procedures and criteria;
3) Use of "crony-based" decision-making systems for hiring and promotion;
4) Presence of a "national search" fetish;
5) Restrictions against hiring one's own graduates;
6) Continuing formal and informal use of nepotism policies;
7) Lack of adequate employment, remuneration, and upward mobility systems for part-time scholars;
8) Isolation, absence or segregation of women in academic affairs;
9) Unequal distribution of work to women.

There is some evidence that different, or at least stricter, criteria seem to be applied to women. For example, much is made of the lower Ph.D. rate for women faculty as an explanation for their lower status. Yet at Quality I institutions (the top colleges and universities as classified by the Carnegie Commission's 1969 National Survey of Higher Education), a higher percentage of the men with only B.A.'s are full professors (23 percent) than are women of those with Ph.D.'s (15 percent) (Freeman 1977).

Similarly, according to Lionel Lewis, "publish or perish" is a myth at all but the top dozen institutions. He claims that the publish or perish dogma is actually a "protective device to conceal the true reasons why someone is forced to leave a department," and that it "promotes the idea that an objective standard is utilized in arriving at decisions which are made subjectively" (Lewis 1975). This may be less true today, as retrenchment at many institutions has made tenure and promotion harder to earn. However, Cole did find that for "silent scientists," those who had not published anything since receiving their Ph.D.'s, women held lower rank and were in less prestigious departments than were men. It seems that women perish more due to lack of publications, while men gain more from productivity.

Affirmative Action

Despite all of these persisting problems, and despite relatively small gains for women faculty since *Academic Women* was published, the general picture has brightened in some ways for women. Both governmental and educational institutions have taken some steps to respond to the issue of discrimination. Federal regulations have been enacted, such as the Equal Pay Act of 1963, requiring equal pay for equal work; Executive Order 11246 as amended by Executive Order 11375, prohibiting discrimination in employment by employers with federal contracts and requiring affirmative action; Title VII of the Civil Rights Act of 1964, as amended by the Equal Employment Opportunity Act of 1972, prohibiting employment discrimination in any public or private educational institution; and Title IX of the Educational Amendments of 1972, forbidding sex discrimination against students and employees in federally assisted programs in institutions which receive federal funding in some form. While enforcement has been sporadic at best, and the current administration does not offer much support for these programs, the very existence of these laws has served as a threat of sorts, motivating institutions to be more active in seeking out women, and to treat them more fairly. While no clear improvements in status for women has resulted, at least major institutions are now forced to consider the equity issue. Given their demonstrated unwillingness to do this on their own over the past few centuries, this is an important, though small, step in the right direction. Bernice Sandler, the Director of the Project on the Status of Women, observed, "Once the law was on the books, women could say that something was unfair, but they could also say that it was illegal, too" (Fields 1982). The Committee on the Education and Employment of Women in Science and Engineering found that "the threat of possible litigation through individual and class action suits, and the cost of such litigation, is probably the most effective enforcement mechanism that exists." What is lacking, however, is a sincere commitment on the part of institutions, both educational and governmental, reflected in vigorous, consistent, and ongoing activity to insure equal access, opportunity, and treatment for women, and to redress past inequities.

Two of the interviewed faculty women spoke to the effect of actual or possible discrimination suits on departmental decisions regarding women faculty.

> Because we had a big law suit in our department and very bad things were done to women, we really had to reform and P_____ has been really pretty good about tenure and women in the 70's.

> I feel that in these various cases, people learn lessons. I don't even care if a female demands this or demands that or they get promoted for the wrong reason—if someone broke the law or something—I would say "Fine," because what happens is for every woman who gets ahead, where there's a big deal made or something, there might be ten women who end up getting promoted without any spectacle made because people realize that "We don't have any just reason; it's really our prejudice that's doing this," and they project and say, "If this went to a court case, we'd lose." . . . There's reasons for laws, and that's to take people who are basically unreasonable and make them reasonable.

From 1972 to 1983, only 60 sex discrimination cases in academia were heard under the Equal Pay Act or under Title VII of the Civil Rights Act. Of those, only six plaintiffs have won (Cowan 1983). Some of the better-known cases include a salary discrimination suit at City University of New York, in which the University was found to have paid women an average of $1800 less than men per year and was ordered to equalize salaries (Desrusseaux 1984); a class action sex discrimination suit against the University of Minnesota which resulted in the University placing its faculty personnel policies under court jurisdiction until 1989 (Perry 1983); and the unsuccessful promotion and tenure case brought against Cornell University by four faculty members, in which the autonomy of faculty in making these decisions was upheld, and statistics showing lower status of women were found insufficient proof of sex discrimination (Fields 1984a).

Two well-publicized tenure cases of women faculty highlight the subjectivity which is a part of tenure and promotion decisions. In the case at Stanford University, Estelle Freedman, an assistant professor of history, claimed that she was denied tenure because her award-winning research in feminist studies was not valued by the faculty tenure committee (Winkler 1983). At Harvard, Theda Skocpol, a sociologist, charged in an internal grievance that she had been denied tenure because she was a woman. Various sources claimed that her forceful personality was a factor in her department's mixed support for her (Schumer 1981). In both instances, the universities ultimately made an offer of tenure, although both times claiming that new additions to the professor's work, rather than evidence of discrimination, were the cause of the reversals (*Chronicle of Higher Education* 27 July 1983; and Sanger 1985). Both of these cases illustrate the compounded problems faced by women, whose scholarly interests may be seen as less important and valuable, whose social exclusion may be held against them, and whose general performance may be evaluated less favorably. Placed up against the highly confidential, subjective, autonomous, male-dominated decision-making processes which are virtually universal in the academic world, women are clearly at a disadvantage in their likelihood of receiving fair and equal treatment.

There are two current judicial issues which, almost certainly, will have an impact on future charges and findings of sex discrimination. The first is the notion of 'comparable worth,' which holds that men and women should receive equal pay, not only for performing the same work, but also for work involving the same levels of skill and responsibility. For academia, the implication would be that faculty members with similar teaching loads, committee work, research projects, and years of experience should be paid equally, regardless of their field. As demonstrated earlier, there is a wide discrepancy by field in faculty salaries, with women clustered in those fields at the lower end of the spectrum. If the concept of comparable worth were to be applied broadly to colleges and universities, it would mean an equalization of salaries, and a general upgrading for women faculty. However, a federal circuit court ruling against nursing faculty at the University of Washington upheld the University's right to pay different salaries to faculty in different fields, based on the marketplace, which suggests a more narrow application and to some, a vastly lower potential to have an overall impact on women's status (Fields 1984b).

The other judicial issue stems from the case of *Grove City College v. Bell*, in which the Supreme Court found that only those programs which receive direct federal funding are subject to Title IX requirements. Conceivably, this could have grave implications for discrimination cases, if the particular department in question receives no aid. There is wide controversy as to whether the decision only applies to the specific situation in the Grove City case, or whether its effects will be far-reaching. In the meantime, there is bipartisan support for extending antidiscrimination laws to entire institutions which receive federal funding in some form.

Within academia itself, there is great resistance to government intervention in internal procedures, particularly those governing personnel decisions. Despite nearly overwhelming evidence to the contrary, many academics cling to the myth of academia as a meritocracy in which individuals rise and fall based solely on their performance. Additionally, they feel that the only ones equipped to judge that performance are those at the top of the ladder, despite the homogeneity of that group.

Thus affirmative action laws and policies are not seen only as burdensome and unwarranted, but also as challenges to the very basis on which the academic system is built. Those within the system, while paying lip service to the notion of equality, contend that the assessment of quality is far too subtle and complex to be subjected to bureaucratic regulation. One author wrote that institutions of higher education should be exempted from the Equal Pay Act, because he feared it would change universities from merit-based to a civil-service administration (Lester, 1975). Numerous judges have supported this autonomy by refusing to interfere with departmental decisions.

Although most observers of academia refer to the difficulties in determining merit, many are unwilling to acknowledge systematic discrimination against women as one element of that difficulty. They simply see women, as a group or as individuals, as being less meritorious, whether by nature, by performance, or due to the "choices" they have made. Seeing the nature of the lower status of women in that light puts the burden back on them, to try to "make the grade" if they can, rather than on the reevaluation and reformation of the system itself.

Ignored in this analysis, however, is the role that discrimination plays in determining the functions women serve and the "choices" they make. For example, women tend to teach more classroom hours and to spend more time in classroom preparation. They tend to be assigned large, introductory classes rather than advanced research-oriented ones. They tend to be overloaded with committee work and other nonacademic tasks. They tend to be located at institutions and in practitioner-oriented disciplines which lack the intellectual atmosphere and support for scholarly discussion, collaboration, and productivity. Even within research institutions, they are likely to be excluded from those networks which would support and encourage scholarship. They may receive less support for fellowships, grants, and sabbaticals. If they are married and have children, they may be forced to interrupt their careers or work part-time if the institutions or their husbands offer no childcare support.

While status channel inconsistency exists for all faculty, women are systematically forced or encouraged into those channels which are less likely to lead to career success. On the one hand, women are forced into situations in which they are less likely to have the same kinds of achievements as men. On the other, when they do perform in the same ways, they are evaluated more harshly or penalized if their work does not fit into a male-centered perspective. Yet academia persists in its self-perception as a fair, bias-free meritocracy which rewards solely on the quality of contributions, an assessment which does not appear to be supported by most of the available data. One faculty woman observed:

I received the highest student evaluations in the school. But that gets discounted in a review process. It depends on what area you're weak in—that's where the focus goes. The rest gets thrown out. This happens to women and blacks. Someone said to me, "Don't you know that women get reviewed twice?"

It is not surprising that while institutions are required to devote some effort in the area of affirmative action, those efforts can seem less than whole-hearted. Suzanne Howard writes:

> Thus, while university administrators appear to have a heightened awareness of the inferior situation of the women on their campuses and what is needed to better the situation, it is apparent that women themselves are the only ones putting forth the special effort to improve the situation. There is meager evidence that the university administrators, predominantly white males, are pushing for special programs, pressing for affirmative action, fighting for the special interests of women, or seriously exploring organizational and individual self-interest for change.

Some, however, would claim that administrators' lack of real effort behind affirmative action is more than a case of benign neglect, but rather a way of effectively eliminating half the competition. This is then couched in the lofty rhetoric of meritocracy.

> The myths allow academic men to believe in their liberality, equality, and fairness. And more important, they allow academic men to smugly assure themselves that they are successful competitors in a merit system while actually reducing the competition they must face by almost 50 percent . . . The real issue is not fear of mediocrity or the potential destruction of the so-called merit system. The real issue is fear that white males will go jobless. [Abramson 1975]

This fear held by some white males of being penalized by preferential treatment for women and minorities seems to be a groundless one, given the continued dominance of white males in virtually every quantifiable measure of success. In fact, if this dominance has indeed continued to exist, has there been any progress for women at all?

It seems that while some progress has been made, the overall picture has remained the same over the past two decades. While there is a greater pool of women with graduate degrees, women continue to be represented in approximately the same proportion within the professoriate. They are more likely than men to be unemployed, underemployed, or in part-time or nontenure track positions. They are clustered in less-prestigious teaching-oriented institutions. They hold lower rank and have lower tenure rates than men. Overall and at each rank, women continue to have lower salaries than men, with the gap widening as one moves up the academic ladder.

Whether the picture will change when and if sufficient numbers of women fight their way into positions of power is difficult to say. But today, as in 1964, higher education continues to be male-dominated in the distribution and acquisition of rewards. Systematic discrimination in subtle and blatant ways throughout their career paths remains a fact of life for academic women.

TABLE 2.1
Distribution of Women, by institutional type, 1981-1982

	Women's share of faculty jobs
Category I University level*	19.4%
Category IIA College level**	25.8%
Category IIB Bachelor's-degree level***	29.4%
Category III 2-year-college level	37.2%
Category IV Institutions without ranks	36.6%
All categories except IV	24.3%

* institutions that confer at least 15 doctoral degrees annually in at least three disciplines.

** institutions that award degrees beyond the bachelor's degree but not qualify for Category I.

*** institutions that award only the bachelor's degree.

SOURCE: American Association of University Professors, cited in "Nine-Month Faculty Salaries for 1981-82," Chronicle of Higher Education, 7 July 1982, p. 10. Copyright 1986 by the Chronicle of Higher Education. Reprinted with Permission.

TABLE 2.2

Estimated Faculty Salaries, 1983-84, by sex and institutional type, and by sex and discipline

	Public institutions			
	Ph.D.-granting		Comprehensive*	
	average(a)	increase(b)	average(a)	increase(b)
Men	$33,289	5.8%	$29,769	5.2%
Women	$27,357	6.6%	$24,542	5.6%
	2-year		Total	
Men	$26,514	5.2%	$30,168	5.4%
Women	$24,271	5.7%	$25,211	5.9%
	Private institutions			
	Ph.D-granting		Comprehensive*	
Men	$35,537	7.0%	$26,944	6.1%
Women	$29,817	6.4%	$21,883	5.4%
	Bachelor's only		Total	
Men	$23,545	7.0%	$27,504	6.7%
Women	$20,274	7.6%	$22,460	6.6%
	Arts, fine and applied		Business and economics	
Men	$26,896	6.6%	$29,768	5.7%
Women	$22,470	5.9%	$23,673	6.4%
	Engineering		Humanities	
Men	$35,028	7.5%	$28,226	6.0%
Women	$25,948	4.0%	$23,928	7.7%
	Physical education		Science and mathematics	
Men	$26,359	5.7%	$29,742	5.6%
Women	$22,599	5.5%	$22,500	5.6%
	Social sciences		Vocational education	
Men	$28,670	5.5%	$27,184	5.0%
Women	$24,978	5.7%	$24,353	6.6%

* institutions with more than 1500 students, a liberal-arts program, and at least one professional program.
(a) Salary figures are for full professor, associate, assistant, and instructor levels.
(b) Increase of average salary for 1983-84 over average for 1982-83.

SOURCE: Survey for the *Chronicle* by John Minter Associates, cited in "Estimated Faculty Salaries for 1983-84," *Chronicle of Higher Education*, 28 March 1984, p. 26. Copyright 1986 by the *Chronicle of Higher Education*. Reprinted with Permission.

TABLE 2.3
Distribution of Men and Women across Ranks and Institutions, 1981-82

	Women's share of faculty jobs	Distribution Men	Women
Category I			
University level			
Professor	6.5%	44.4%	12.8%
Associate Professor	17.5%	29.3%	25.8%
Assistant Professor	31.4%	21.6%	41.0%
Instructor	54.0%	3.0%	14.3%
Lecturer	46.0%	1.7%	6.1%
All ranks	19.4%	100%	100%
Category IIA			
College level			
Professor	12.3%	37.1%	15.0%
Associate Professor	21.0%	32.4%	24.9%
Assistant Professor	36.6%	24.3%	40.4%
Instructor	53.3%	5.3%	17.6%
Lecturer	44.5%	0.9%	2.1%
All ranks	22.9%	100%	100%
Category IIB			
Bachelor's degree level			
Professor	13.2%	30.1%	11.0%
Associate Professor	38.0%	30.1%	44.3%
Assistant Professor	52.7%	8.2%	21.9%
Instructor	44.3%	0.5%	1.0%
All ranks	29.4%	100%	100%
Category III			
2-year college level			
Professor	22.1%	22.3%	10.7%
Associate Professor	31.5%	31.7%	24.6%
Assistant Professor	40.5%	30.5%	35.1%
Instructor	52.6%	15.3%	28.7%
Lecturer	73.5%	0.2%	0.9%
All ranks	37.2%	100%	100%
All categories			
Professor	9.7%	38.8%	13.0%
Associate Professor	20.6%	30.7%	24.7%
Assistant Professor	35.1%	24.1%	40.6%
Instructor	53.3%	5.2%	19.5%
Lecturer	46.4%	1.2%	3.2%
All ranks	24.3%	100%	100%

SOURCE: American Association of University Professors, cited in "Nine Month Faculty Salaries for 1981-82," *Chronicle of Higher Education*, 7 July 1982, p. 10. Copyright 1986 by the *Chronicle of Higher Education*. Reprinted with Permission.

TABLE 2.4
Tenure Status of Associate Professors Holding Science and Engineering
Ph.D.'s, by Field of Employment and Sex, 1975 and 1977.

| | Number and Percent in Tenured Positions | | | |
| | 1975 | | 1977 | |
Field	Men	Women	Men	Women
All Science and Engineering	25,136	2.097	28,755	2,250
	78.8%	71.3%	81.9%	72.9%
Mathematics	2,573	134	3.098	164
	81.9%	74.9%	88.2%	82.0%
Physics/Astronomy	1,956	35	2,181	31
	81.3%	100%	88.2%	82.0%
Chemistry	2,406	216	2,493	169
	85.4%	78.3%	89.1%	76.1%
Earth Sciences	1,076	23	1,125	18
	68.8%	100%	79.0%	100%
Agricultural Sciences	1,555	12	1,616	12
	82.7%	100%	81.1%	100%
Medical Sciences	800	133	1,612	200
	63.7%	55.0%	67.6%	65.1%
Biological Sciences	4,737	528	5,218	612
	80.1%	72.9%	80.9%	65.9%
Psychology	2,274	422	2,508	485
	70.8%	65.8%	77.6%	70.6%
Social Sciences	4,432	594	5,888	844
	74.4%	73.3%	82.6%	79.4%

SOURCE: Committee on the Education and Employment of Women in Science
and Engineering, *Climbing the Academic Ladder: Doctoral Women Scientists in
Academe* (Washington: National Academy of Sciences, 1979), p. 84.

3
Teachers Versus
Women-of-Knowledge

Publication is the only way a man can communicate with a
significant number of colleagues or other adults. Those who do
not publish usually feel they have not learned anything worth
communicating to adults. This means they have not learned
much worth communicating to the young either.

—Jencks and Riesman (1968)

Once it was obvious that there was a so-called feminization of
the professorial role and women were going into the academic
scene, then the hierarchy of what was most respected or admired
or rewarded just became a little bit different, more subtle, so
that you have these kinds of oppositions between women who
teach. Women teach, men do research. That's the very obvious
one. Another one is that women teach language while men teach
literature. It's a very standard situation. The finally more subtle
one is women who do certain kinds of research, as opposed to
men, and of course the problem of women being segregated into
women's studies . . . So there is always the hierarchy and there
are, of course, always women at every step to challenge the
hierarchy, but it's very real.

—interview with a faculty woman

In the institutional hierarchy of academia, one of the most important indices of status is what activities are expected, supported,
valued, and rewarded for professors. The most important element
of the hierarchy is the dichotomy between teaching and research.
As a rule, the most prestigious institutions tend to reward schol-

51

arship over teaching with salary increments, promotion, and tenure. Research performance is easier to quantify and evaluate than teaching performance, and has a wider and more direct impact on the general intellectual community than even the most inspiring lecture given to a class of undergraduates. Even lesser institutions, while realizing that many of their faculty will never be as prolific as world-renowned scholars, value and reward research productivity. This is even more true as the academic job crunch makes it possible for less elite institutions to attract topnotch faculty who may have been unavailable to them decades earlier.

Among faculty members themselves, there are several factors which influence whether the role of teacher or researcher is to be emphasized. One set involves the interests, preferences, and abilities of the faculty member. Another involves the demands, rewards, and supports within his or her institution, discipline, occupational level, and greater social and personal context.

Jessie Bernard divided faculty into two categories: teachers and 'men-of-knowledge.' The distinction is a more subtle one than that between teaching and research or between institutional or disciplinary loyalty. It is related instead to the way in which one sees oneself in relation to the subject matter, the students, and other scholars in the field. She wrote: "The role of the teacher, in brief, is to serve as an instrument of communication; the role of the man of knowledge is to serve as a collaborator with the original author." It is implicit in the very terminology that 'men-of-knowledge' are almost exclusively male, with women more likely to fall into the 'teacher' category.

Even within the teaching role, Bernard found differences between men and women. When controversies came up, she claimed that women were dismissed as lacking the knowledge, authority, and perspective necessary to convey information or points of view over which there was some dispute. She cited several studies of actual teaching effectiveness which showed women being praised for their thoroughness and concern for students, rather than their brilliance or insight.

In a study in which a man and a woman gave identical lectures to undergraduates, the students retained the same amount of material, but were less likely to accept it as fact when the woman was the speaker (unpublished study, Penn. State University, 1958). These results, along with other findings and general observations, led Bernard to question whether women, on the average, could be as effective overall as men in teaching, as the recipients would benefit less due to their own inability to accept and respect the competence and authority of a woman in an unconventional role. She wrote:

> Role theory states that roles are always reciprocal, that their performance always involves a mutual response: Roles cannot be performed alone, in isolation. No matter how well one person performs his role, if the other person or persons do not respond, the role is not, in effect, being performed at all. The success of any role performance depends, therefore, as much on Alter's performance of the complementary role as it does on Ego's performance of his role. Thus the question may well be raised, quite apart from their intellectual qualifications, whether women, no matter how well trained they are or how skillful, actually do for students as teachers what men do.

This issue of mutual response in the evaluation of role performance reemerged throughout the discussion of the various roles women faculty played. The subjectivity inherent in making assessments on such factors as teaching effectiveness, research quality or advising makes it difficult to have a sense of the true nature of women's performance of any of these roles. For this reason, the discussion of women as men-of-knowledge tends to focus on easily quantifiable measures such as types and quantities of research publications, although the attitudes of the evaluator have an impact there as well.

Another factor listed by Bernard in the definition of a man-of-knowledge was the willingness and ability to play the required social role. Being an innovator requires, by definition, that one challenge the status quo and battle active or passive resistance to get one's ideas to the forefront. One must be prepared for, or even relish, the spotlight and have confidence in one's abilities and one's work. None of these behaviors are consistent with the traditional female role.

> The innovative role is an instrumental one and not consonant with the emotional-expressive role assigned to women in most societies. Women are socialized into a role whose function is conserving, stabilizing, appeasing.

This is compounded by the fact that women's contributions can be ignored or overlooked, simply because they are made by women.

Once again, the reciprocity of roles enters the picture, for if the evaluator does not or cannot recognize innovation, has it occurred? Bernard felt that women's contributions tended to be buried under a blanket of neglect. In some areas, women faced open resistance and rejection, as they were not considered qualified to comment on various societal phenomena, such as industrial sociology or military history. In others, they were not taken seriously, as they did not fit the image of the profession. In some cases, discoveries made by men and women were credited to the men, or ideas proposed by men and women more easily accepted when delivered by men. She wrote:

> If, as noted above, acceptance of new ideas is difficult when they are presented by aggressive, ambitious, competitive men, it is even more difficult when they are presented by women, whom we are not used to seeing in the idea-man or instrumental role. We are simply not used to looking for innovation and originality from women.

In 1964, while the role of academic women may have been nontraditional, Bernard perceived that women performed traditional functions within that role. They tended to be conservers and transmitters of knowledge and culture, rather than bold innovators at the far-reaches of their disciplines. They tended to be noted for attentive and concerned relationships with their students, rather than for initiating them into the rigors of their profession. Even when their actual behavior fell outside of these demarcations, it tended not to be recognized and valued as such. In short, whether due to cultural, environmental, or social factors, Bernard contended that women stayed within the confines of a traditional women's role. Is this still true today?

Teaching versus Research

Much current research points to the fact that women continue to be more heavily involved in teaching than research. For almost every cohort of the 13,487 faculty members who responded to an American Council on Education survey in 1972, male faculty were more likely than women to list research as their principal activity, while female faculty were more likely to list teaching (Tuckman 1979).

The contrast is more dramatic in comparing the results of the A.C.E. survey in 1972 with a survey of the Higher Education Research Institute in 1980. In 1980, 10.9 percent of the women faculty members reported spending 17 hours or more per week in teaching, as opposed to 7.5 percent of the men, while 13.2 percent of the men and 7.0 percent of the women spent 21 hours or more per week doing research. While the proportion of men in the heavy research category stayed constant from 1972, the proportion of women went up 1.7 percent, which indicates that the gap may be narrowing (Astin and Snyder 1982).

Bernard felt that the teacher/man-of-knowledge distinction went beyond simple time spent teaching or conducting research. It was also reflected in the numbers and types of courses taught, with teachers being located primarily at the elementary levels of disciplines. Again, women tend to be teachers; 34.9 percent of women versus 22.4 percent of men teach entirely undergraduate students, while a greater proportion of men than women teach entirely graduate students (15.9 percent of men, 11 percent of women) (Centra 1974).

Whatever the explanation, women seem to devote more time to teaching and less to research, and this results in lower rates of publication relative to men. One analysis of matched pairs of male and female scientists found that over a twelve-year career, the median publication rate was eight papers for men and three for women (Cole 1979). A study of 92 marketing faculty showed that 49.5 percent of the men, compared to 30.9 percent of the women, had three or more publications, while 46.9 percent of the women, and only 31.9 percent of the men, had none (Robertson 1979). A study of sociology journals showed that while the publishing record of women had improved significantly from 1967 to 1973, when the percentage of articles with female authorship rose from 15.6 percent to 23.6 percent, women were still absent from three quarters of the publishing in 14 journals in the field (Mackie 1977). These trends even begin to emerge among graduate students, where one study showed 42.1 percent of the male students in bacteriology and 38.7 percent in chemistry had published an article, compared to 26.4 percent and 24.6 percent respectively for women (Feldman 1974). Of course, in examining these data one must consider the differences between male and female graduate students in the opportunity, support, and sponsorship they receive for their research. One must also be cautious in generalizing from these statistics, given the small number of women in these fields.

Why is this the case? The greater likelihood that women do not have a doctorate, are at lower ranks, or at teaching institutions certainly comes into play. Additionally, department chairs and deans may consciously or unconsciously hold the assumption that women are most appropriate in elementary teaching roles, and assign them accordingly.

Another possible and often-cited explanation is that women prefer and actively choose the role of teacher. There is some evidence within the current research to support this. Feldman's study of faculty and graduate students found women far more likely to report a strong orientation towards teaching than men for almost every field. Centra found women significantly more likely to be primarily interested in teaching (32.5 percent of the women versus 25.6 percent of the men). Despite the differences, however, it should be noted that overall the majority of men are somewhat more interested in teaching than research (64.5 percent) in a proportion only 8 percent less than women, while only a 6 percent smaller proportion of women (24.2 percent) than men (30.2 percent) somewhat favor research. Thus, while the difference between the sexes is apparent, the image that all academic men are busily exploring new areas while academic women are only comfortable in the classroom is by no means an accurate one.

Interestingly, among women interviewed for this study, a contrary trend emerged. Of the twenty women, eight said they preferred research and writing, seven liked them equally, one was primarily an administrator, and only four preferred teaching. All of the women enjoyed both a great deal, and saw an important interrelationship between the two.

One of the women described the important balance between the tension and excitement of the woman-of-knowledge role and the security and comfort of the teacher role.

> Graduate teaching complements research. Research is very frustrating because you're always on the border of what is not known and so you become very insecure because you see all this stuff that you don't know, whereas in the classroom you try to tell people that this is the key way to think about everything so it all fits together, but you're talking about what is known. Maybe it's nice to have both together, because one keeps the other sane.

In answer to the question of whether they preferred teaching or research, the following three women, who preferred research, also addressed the interconnectedness of the two:

Research, but I don't think they're mutually exclusive. My research makes me a better teacher . . . There's a lot of pressure in the academic world to say you're better in one or the other, but ideally you're better in each because you do the other.

Research and writing. I love my teaching and I don't like to say this because it kind of downgrades my teaching. I think my teaching benefits from my research, contrary to what some people say.

Research and scholarship. I don't say it too loud, too often, but I teach to support my scholarship habit . . . I'm fortunate that I teach the things I write about, so that there's not a big gap between what I'm doing in my scholarly life and what I'm doing in my teaching life.

Similarly, two of the women who preferred teaching also mentioned the pleasure they received from their scholarly work. It is interesting to note that these two women were among the most senior of the sample, both having been at the university for more than ten years.

I love teaching. I love being with students. I don't think you can be a really good teacher without doing research—you're stale—and I just like doing research. I get excited about what I'm teaching. The teaching stimulates research—it's not the research that stimulates the teaching.

Well now, of course, it's the teaching. I enjoy working with the students very much. I enjoy it most in a research setting.

Two of the women who indicated that the majority of their time went into research activities claimed that they were motivated by an awareness of the prestige and reward system that more highly values research.

I very consciously try to put myself into the research category. Whether I've succeeded is another question.

I would like to think of myself probably as both, and right now, at my age—this is the beginning of my fourth year

> on staff and the tenure issue is looming very large—I
> found myself gearing more towards research and sort of
> paying less emphasis to the teaching . . . I think that is
> sort of a necessary evil of the system. But my motivation
> now is very different from my first year, when I was very
> gung-ho.

Of course, it should not be surprising that women at a research-oriented, elite institution would themselves be oriented towards research. However, as women continue to be more highly represented at institutions which do not emphasize research, such as two-year colleges and colleges and universities of less elite status, and in departments which are practitioner or nonresearch-oriented, their publication rates continue to be lower. It is difficult to ascertain whether they chose such positions to reinforce their personal preferences, as Bernard suggested, or whether the lack of rewards and professional stimulation in their institutional environment led to their lower overall rates. There does seem to be a relationship between academic career plans of graduate students and interest in teaching or research, but it is difficult to know which came first (Feldman). Also, because many of these graduate students will not realize their aspirations, it would be interesting to assess the effect of their actual institutional affiliation on their research activity.

Even within Quality I institutions, however, the publication rates of women are lower, with 68 percent of the women, compared to 51 percent of the men, publishing no books, and 38 percent of the women, compared to 15 percent of the men, no articles. Twenty percent of the men, compared to 10 percent of the women, had published three or more books, and 45 percent of the men, compared to 17 percent of the women had published 11 or more articles. While some of this difference is attributable to the greater practitioner-orientation of the departments in which women tend to be located, even within those departments, women published less (Freeman 1977).

Although such factors as institutional affiliation, possession of the doctorate, discipline, and personal preference continue to have an effect on the productivity of women, other factors may have an influence as well. Some of these include the relationships between the social roles that women are likely to play both generally and as faculty members. In Bernard's terminology, women are more likely to serve emotional-expressive functions than instrumental ones, meaning that they are more likely to be concerned with others' well-being than with tangible activities and accomplishments. This may manifest itself in personal, rather than purely intellectual, relationships with students.

This tendency towards more personalized interaction was evident even among the highly research-oriented faculty interviewed for this study, who derived great satisfaction from their ability to help individual students. Yet for one professor, those positive feelings seemed to be tinged by an awareness that the students were likely to view them as being more concerned and supportive than men, and to take advantage of it.

> They make more demands on me and that's becoming less true as I get older and meaner and sterner. I have always known that they don't respect my time as much as they respect that of men in the department who are much less busy than I am. I mean, they don't write as much, they don't speak as much, they don't work as hard. And yet there is a feeling on the part of many of our students that male time is sacrosanct and female time is theirs. And they're more familiar with me. They assume a kind of benevolence on my part, and I gather from speaking to them that on the part of many men, they assume a kind of sternness and awe and authoritarianism, which is not true of these guys. I'm really much more authoritarian than a lot of the men, but they're cozier with me in a way that can be very annoying.

For another, the students perceptions seemed accurate.

> They probably think that I care for them more. They probably think I'm more sensitive than the awful men around here. [Are you?] Oh yeah!

This orientation towards personal in addition to purely intellectual interactions seems evident in the accounts of several of the faculty women, who told of students seeking them out to discuss personal as well as academic concerns, with one saying, "I think that they feel they can talk to me about a lot of things that are maybe bothering them." Yet for others, this willingness to be accessible to students for individual attention seemed counterproductive to becoming women-of-knowledge. In one case, the faculty member seemed torn by conflicting expectations, and by a sense of responsibility to her students, even when it did not seem to be in her own best interest.

> So yes, I prefer research. No, I cannot say that since coming to P_____ my major efforts have been in research, and it's bothering me immensely. And it's not so easy—there is standard advice both to new faculty and to women—"You don't have to spend so much time with students." But in my case, often because they're foreign students, they really do need time . . . I've spent a lot of time and I'm trying to curtail it. At this point, I am in the midst of trying to regain a balance.

There is little empirical data documenting whether women actually spend more time than men in individual advising, or whether they spend their time with students in different ways than men. One could speculate, however, that both would be the case. First, women are more likely to be found at institutions, such as small women's colleges and church-affiliated schools, which value and encourage individualized student attention. Second, not only may some faculty women be more able and willing to play that function than men, but perhaps students are more likely to see and respond to them in that light, given the supportive function women generally play in society. Again, the notion of role reciprocity is important. If students perceive women as being more concerned with their emotional well-being, then they may seek them out to discuss personal concerns, resulting in women spending more time in those types of conversations.

Conversely, Bernard felt that women may not be willing or able to play the necessary social role to be women-of-knowledge. The role seems to require a strong competitive drive, a sense of comfort with the spotlight and with having one's work closely scrutinized, and a deep sense of confidence in one's abilities and work. The current research seems to lend some support to Bernard's contention.

One study showed that women tend to rate themselves lower than men. In response to a questionnaire sent to all full-time faculty at two universities, the men evaluated themselves significantly higher than the women on their reputation as a teacher, their research productivity, and their professional reputation, with little relationship between the women's self-rating and their actual standing with respect to their colleagues. This study found no difference between men and women in their level of ambition or their assessment of their intelligence (Widom and Burke 1978).

In another study, female graduate students in five scientific disciplines were less likely than their male counterparts to agree with the statement, "I hope to make significant contributions to knowledge in my field." They also seemed to be less confident in their ability to do original work. Among graduate students, women were less likely to rate themselves as being among the best in their departments and they were more likely to see themselves as students than as scholar-scientists (Feldman). Another study showed that women needed to spend more time than men in their academic programs to develop ambition for scholarly eminence (Acker 1977).

Women and men also seem to have different indicators of academic self-esteem. An A.C.E. survey of faculty at four-year institutions showed that for men, association with a research institution rather than a teaching one is related to their self-esteem. For women, high self-esteem in comparison to men was correlated with support of women-related issues and with teaching effectiveness. However, in relation to other women, self-esteem was related to an association with male faculty who felt more successful than other men. "These women have made an important but subtle substitution: it is the institutional association with elite men, rather than the institutional commitment to research, to which the feelings of being more successful than other women are related" (Tidball 1976). This suggests that in comparing themselves to men, women value themselves for those contributions which are uniquely theirs, namely women's issues. In comparison to other women, they may be more likely to rate themselves by male standards of status, which seem to closely mirror the spectrum of institutional status within higher education.

However, these phenomena may in fact be symptoms rather than causes of women's greater likelihood of being teachers as opposed to men of knowledge. If women are the victims of discrimination in the receipt of financial, intellectual, and emotional support to do research, they are not as likely as men to have confidence in their research ability. If they are less likely to be perceived and treated as if they were among the best graduate students, it is not surprising that they would rate themselves lower than their male counterparts. Given that they may not receive the same encouragement as men, it stands to reason that it would take them longer to develop ambition for scholarly eminence. Thus, while these studies do support, to an extent, the notion that women are less likely than men to have the confidence, self-image and motivation to do research, I would argue that this is the result of discrimination, not a justification for the inequity which exists.

Evaluation of Women

Numerous studies reveal that, at least within some realms, women's work is rated lower than men's. For example, in one study, 368 college students evaluated a job application and samples of newspaper writing. Half of the students were told that the applicant was male; the other half were told the applicant was female. The competence of the female journalist was devalued on all eight items of evaluation, with the men judging her more harshly than the women. The male students saw the male journalist as being significantly more professionally competent, as having a greater likelihood of job success, and as having written an article with more value for the reader (Etaugh and Kasley 1981).

Similarly, in another study, male and female undergraduates were asked to evaluate faculty members, designated as male and female, on the basis of identical descriptions of their teaching methods and practices. The female students rated the male and female professors equally, while the males rated the men higher on the factors of effectiveness, concern, likeableness, and excellence. Both the males and females rated the men as having more power (Kaschak 1978). Another study in which undergraduates evaluated actual teaching effectiveness showed that male, but not female, students evaluated female social science instructors lower than male instructors, although less so if the women also exhibited "feminine" traits, such as friendliness, smiling, and eye contact (Martin 1984).

In a similar study, there were no differences in the way the subjects judged essays attributed to men and women in traditional women's fields. However, male subjects devalued the work of women in traditionally male fields, unless the women were said to have a Ph.D. Female subjects did not devalue the work of women in male fields; in fact, they rated the work of female doctorates higher than that of male doctorates (Isaacs 1981).

In another study, undergraduates evaluated an article on a sex-neutral topic written by an author who was designated as male or female, and as having high professional status, as an associate professor, or low status, as a a graduate student. In general, the high status authors received more positive evaluations than the low status ones. This was even more dramatic for the female subjects, who rated the high status women more favorably and the low status women more negatively than did the male subjects (Peck 1978).

These studies indicate that for women more than men, tangible indicators of status have an influence in the way in which they, and their work, are perceived. Women apparently need external validation of some sort before they are taken seriously. The notion of reciprocity of roles reemerges, for the actual merit of the author's work becomes lost if the receiver does not perceive it. Women must prove themselves twice—first, their own authority and competence and then, the value of their work.

Several of the women interviewed for this study reported perceiving changes in the responses they received from students when they crossed some sort of status line, moving from not authoritative to authoritative. For one, it came with the receipt of the doctorate. Before that, she perceived a tendency to be discounted by male students. She observed:

> And I've also noticed that new students that didn't know me before—Freshmen—if I were just Miss _____, might treat me one way and now that I'm Dr. _____, they're not really sure where I'm coming from and somehow that gives another level of credence to what I'm saying. I think the male students have a tendency, particularly in the past, to write you off . . . The first year you start teaching you really have to prove yourself. Somehow or another I don't feel that anymore, but they make you feel that you need—it's like—"Well, I'm going to sit back," and "Show me that you've got anything." Or sometimes not that at all—sometimes they're not interested in anything you have to say.

For others, it came with age and experience.

> I think, especially during the first years when I was much younger, some students at least might have had a bit less

confidence, not necessarily in my quality or in my competence, but certainly in my authority and in the power I carried. I didn't have any power, and that is a serious consideration for a graduate student.

When I first came to P _____, a number of times I had male students who had a lot of trouble dealing with a female teacher. Now I think partly the students have changed, and I'm a lot older, so I just come across sufficiently authoritative or something.

For minority women, this challenging of their authority may be compounded by racism. One black faculty woman recalled:

The students make assumptions about you and about who you are. It has to do more with intensity of responses. You are tested more; you are challenged more. For a minority instructor, you get tested over and over. Even at the end of two semesters with students, someone will have the audacity to stand up and challenge you. They wouldn't with a white instructor.

The studies showed that women are evaluated less favorably when they step outside of traditionally feminine areas of knowledge. One faculty member in this study had difficulty with some of her students when she taught quantitative material.

I did have some trouble last year in one class. I was teaching a very mathematical, quantitative, technical course and they weren't understanding it and I do think some of their frustration was at a female trying to teach them something that they thought was a male subject and them not able to handle it. I do think there was some sexism involved.

Another discovered that she was being perceived in a traditionally feminine role, even though she did not feel that her behavior merited it.

I was team-teaching with a colleague of mine, a friend of mine, a black man—physically very big and I'm small, and very dark with a big voice—and we hadn't talked about that part of our relationship at all. We'd talk a lot about the course and planned it, and we'd talk about how his area of competence was in psychology and mine was in economics and social policy and how that was going to fit together, and what we realized after a week or two of the class was that that was not how the class was seeing us. They were seeing us as a big black man and a weak little white woman who was not going to be able to protect them at all. That was strange and it took a while for me to try to be very aggressive and nasty in class to disaffect them of that role.

These phenomena would necessarily have an impact on the reputation of women faculty. Jonathan Cole, in his study of the reputation and perceived quality of the work of male and female scientists found this to be the case. In a survey asking 2,162 randomly chosen scientists to name the five most important contributors to their fields over the past decade, women comprised 3 percent of those listed in psychology and sociology and 2 percent of those listed in biology, although they comprised 10 to 25 percent of the lists from which the subjects worked. Interestingly, women were far more likely to name other women; 45 percent of the female sociologists named women compared to 17 percent of the males, while 50 percent of the female psychologists named women versus 17 percent of the males (Cole).

Based on further responses to the same survey, in which the listed scientists were rated on the quality and visibility of their research contributions, the scientists were divided into four reputational types—prominent (widely known and highly regarded), notorious (widely known but poorly regarded), esteemed (highly regarded but not widely known), and invisible (neither highly regarded nor known). Thirty-eight percent of the men, but only 19 percent of the women were in the prominent category; 13 percent of the women and 8 percent of the men were in the notorious category; 56 percent of the women, but only 37 percent of the men were in the invisible category.

It seems that women and their work are much less regarded and known than men and their work. Further analysis of the data shows that women scientists are known to 8 percent fewer members of their disciplines than are males in comparably rated departments; that women are known 9 percent less frequently than men from comparable doctoral departments; and that women are known 8 percent less frequently than men with the same number of honorific awards.

These data illustrate the flaws in the argument that if women performed equally to men, they would be deserving of and would receive equal recognition and esteem. Men, who make up the majority of the faculty ranks, seem to have difficulty even "seeing" the work of women, much less evaluating it as equal to their own and that of their male colleagues. It would follow that men would not be likely to cite women's scholarship in their own research, decreasing its chances for visibility even further. This illustrates that what may seem like an objective and unbiased explanation of the lesser reputation of women—that their reputations equal their actual performance—may in fact mask the true discrimination which occurs in women's careers. If, as the research shows, women are evaluated less favorably than men, particularly by men, then their access to the woman-of-knowledge role contains obstacles every step of the way.

Women's Scholarship

Another element in the perception of research by women is that the work is frequently on issues of particular importance to women, or that the work may be published in a feminist, and therefore presumably lesser, journal. Academic men habitually judge work through the eyes of their own seldom-challenged experiences and scholarly traditions. They themselves have been trained in a "system that prepares men to take up roles of power in man-centered society, that asks questions and teaches 'facts' generated by a male intellectual tradition, and that both subtly and openly confirms men as the leaders and shapers of human destiny, both within and outside academia" (Rich 1975). The result is a world view in which the lives and experiences of half of the population are seen as being of lesser importance, if their distinctiveness is noted at all, or are seen solely in their relationship to men. This trivialization of women's experiences would almost necessarily lead to a trivialization of research and writing on them. The assessment of women-related scholarship by men, who are far more likely to be in position in which their judgment matters, would inevitably be less favorable. Bernard (1982) wrote:

There is another relative factor subverting rational universalistic criteria in judging the work of women researchers, namely the fact that a considerable amount of it in recent times deals with subjects which are of little interest to men, with which they are not even acquainted and the quality of which they are in no position to judge. To them it looks trivial, dull, off-beat, banal. They do not know how to fit it into their tight little parochial system. Much of it is not welcome in establishment journals. Prejudice, ignorance, and parochialism may thus easily subvert universalistic criteria in the distribution of rewards.

Similarly, one faculty woman interviewed for this study stated:

If you would sort of survey the general population at P____, both faculty and students, you would have individual people telling you that women are equal and as capable as men. But that gets muddied a lot when actual decisions are made. My perception and feeling is that it's most problematic when women work on the issues of women's culture, women's interests—that sort of thing. The way status is made problematic for women is to question the area of women's research and say that that is not an area in and of itself; it's not a discipline; it's secondary work.

The absence of women from the content of scholarship occurs in a number of ways. The major issues of disciplines may be defined in such a way that women are necessarily absent. This is true, for example, of those disciplines which focus on public life, such as religion, political science, or history, because women have often been active in private, rather than public, spheres. The absence of women in official leadership roles within societal institutions has been given as the explanation for their absence in much of the literature in the field. This is not to suggest that these disciplines have appropriately excluded women, or that their self-definition is a natural and correct one, but rather that men have tended to elevate their own interests, lives, and accomplishments as the only ones worthy of study. One political scientist wrote:

The complication here is that there never was any way that the modern study of politics could fail to be sexist.

Its empirical concerns have been almost exclusively those
of the exercise of public power, aspects of political elites,
and aspects of the institutions of government. Such studies are bound to exclude women, largely because women
usually do not dispose of public power, belong to political
elites or hold influential positions in government institutions. [Lovenduski 1981]

Questioning not only the male-centeredness of her discipline, but
the fact that it is seldom challenged, another political scientist
asked:

Why should this radical asymmetry by sexes not itself
have been a research problem of the first magnitude for
the discipline throughout the years? Why, that is, was it
consistently taken for granted that men and not women
should populate the public sphere, and why did so few
observers stop to meditate upon this fascinating fact?
[Keohane 1982]

Similarly, those events and issues which disciplines choose to
study also tend to be those within the male rather then the female
realm. Economists may choose to study the productivity of farmers
while ignoring the productivity of farm wives. Labor historians may
focus on male factory workers and ignore domestic workers. Psychologists may form theories of achievement motivation, but not
of the desire to nurture. Literary critics have overlooked works written by women, or have neglected to analyze the depiction of wom-
en's experience within texts written by men. These are but a few
examples of the way in which disciplines shape an intellectual world
in which the experiences and contributions of women are absent
either through neglect or outright denial of their importance.

Further, if men have a view of the world in which women are
functionally invisible, then they would tend to generalize their own
experiences to include both men and women, whether or not it was
appropriate. The result is a body of knowledge which is based, at
best, on half truths. These assumptions color the way research is
constructed and understood, as men are considered the population
to be studied, analyzed, and described to arrive at truth. Helen Roberts (1981) writes: "To those whose methodology is suffused with
sexism in this way, a sample composed entirely of men is seen as

unproblematical, while one composed entirely of women may be seen as odd, inadequate, or perverse." An example of this can be found in a study of the choice of sex of subjects in research in psychology. All authors of articles published in *Journal of Personality and Social Psychology* in 1970 and 1971 were asked what guided their choice of subjects. Five reasons were given for not using men, while 26 were given for not using women, such as poor subject cooperation, lower dependability of scoring, and potential embarrassment for women. Only two of the 41 respondents who gave explanations did so in their articles. In fact, 70 percent of the time, the authors failed to mention that male subjects were used, while authors mentioned that only females were used in more than half of the cases. In the articles using only one sex, 92 percent of the all-male findings were generalized to women, while only 60 percent of the all-female findings were generalized to men (Prescott 1978).

Similarly, it is not uncommon for sociological and economic studies to classify married women's social class as that of her husband's, regardless of her own occupation, and to classify married women as having no occupation if they are unpaid homemakers (Delphy 1981). Carol Gilligan's book, *In a Different Voice,* contends that Laurence Kohlberg's stages of moral development are based solely on analysis of the experiences of males, ignoring differences in male and female imagery of relationships, through which women see them as webs of interconnection rather than the hierarchies which males envision. In philosophy, ways of understanding that are more typical of men are seen as universal, while those of women are rarely considered or valued. One philosopher wrote:

> Men and women express their consciousness not only in *what* they think, but *how* they think. Men think, perceive, select, argue, justify malely. *What* they have thought, *how* they have thought, world-views and Lebenswelten imbedded necessarily in a male consciousness, become manifest in their intellectual constructions, their philosophies. That is perhaps how it should be. What should not be is the raising of these male constructs so that women cannot 'legitimately' think, perceive, select, argue, etc. from their unique stance. [Ruth 1981]

These issues are magnified for minority women—by sex, ethnicity, sexual orientation, or disability. In the same way that women are assumed to be slightly deficient, slightly abnormal men, minority women are subsumed under majority women in most academic treatments. In those areas in which they are clearly different, these differences are seen as problems or weaknesses. The experiences of minority women are viewed through the distorted lens of the majority culture and values regardless of whether they are applicable.

For example, the experiences, contributions, and ideas of black women are virtually invisible in all of the traditional disciplines, and often receive secondary prominence in both Afro-American studies and women's studies. When they are depicted or described, it is often in limited and even inaccurate ways. Patricia Bell Scott contends that black women are absent from studies of American society and human behavior, seen within a narrow problem-oriented perspective, and described from a framework which has not been updated for forty years (Scott 1982).

This same invisibility is true of lesbians, who—while undoubtedly present in any group of women being examined—are absent from virtually all scholarly analysis. Not only are their own achievements and contributions sometimes ignored, but they are further pushed aside by heterosexist intellectual constructs which see women primarily in terms of their relationships to significant males, such as husbands or sons. Work on lesbian-related topics may be further inhibited by apprehension about homophobic reactions from those evaluating it.

More complex than the absence of women from the content of traditional disciplines is the impact of male dominance on research itself. Male values and characteristics define the stated and unstated values and characteristics of scholarship, with an emphasis on objectivity, distance, competition, and control. For example, Evelyn Fox Keller suggests that primary goals of male-defined science are control and domination over nature (1983). Others claim that social science data gathering is often based on strict distance from those being studied. One author contends that the textbook definition of "proper" interview technique owes "a great deal more to a masculine social and sociological vantage point than to a feminine one" and "appeals to such values as objectivity, detachment, hierarchy, and 'science' as an important cultural activity which takes priority over people's more individualized concerns" (Oakley 1981). "Hard" data, or that which can be quantified, is seen as more valuable than "soft," or more descriptive, data. It is clear that male-centered assumptions about the "proper" conceptualization, implementation, and presentation of research have implications for all research, not just that related specifically to issues of gender. All of these forces combine to have a far-reaching impact on academia and on the women within it. Because research on women is perceived as being outside of the mainstream, biased, political, unimportant, and/or inaccurate, women whose interests and work lie in this area are at an obvious disadvantage in being published. This may be especially true if they challenge time-honored male-centered traditions and assumptions. The fact that much of this research reaches print through feminist publishers and journals further reinforces its image as political work on the fringes of scholarship, unable to meet the standards of its field.

Women are also disadvantaged to the extent that they are forced to work through a male perspective. Of course, all of their academic, and indeed their societal, experience has been in this tradition, so it is not a foreign one. However, the fit may not be as natural for them as it is for their male colleagues. Further, the inception of research questions often comes from observations and puzzles from the researcher's own life. Women may be less likely or able to use their own experience as a stimulus, unless they translate their ideas into a more acceptable male-centered framework.

In turn, this inhibits the development of a full body of scholarship by women, as their contributions and perspectives are not allowed to flourish as are men's. Nor are their ideas given the same analysis and criticism; they are dismissed without careful consideration. The final outcome is a skewed and incomplete world view, reflected in both academia and society at large.

Over the past two decades, however, feminist scholarship has grown in size and recognition. One group of authors defines it as "scholarship with a recognizably feminist analytical perspective on the oppression and liberation of women" (DuBois et al. 1985). Another group suggests that it is "a commitment to undoing polarities—between conceptions of the sexes, between academic disciplines, between the academic and political communities, between theory and experiences, and between the postures of objectivity and subjectivity" (Abel and Abel 1983). Still others see it simply as that work which takes women into account, in incorporating their perspectives and ways of knowing and behaving into the research process and in judging their lives and experiences worthy of study. It has taken many forms—both compensatory, to fill in the gaps in traditional scholarship, and innovative, to apply feminist perspectives and inquiry to all scholarship.

One manifestation of the growth of feminist scholarship has been the rapid increase in women's studies curricula throughout the country. Growing from only fifteen in 1972 to over 500 a decade later, with approximately 100 institutions offering degrees, it has become a visible, if not fully accepted, part of many campuses over a relatively short period of time (Williams et al. 1983). It is estimated that there are 30,000 women's studies courses being taught in American institutions (Boxer 1982). In the same vein, there are approximately 50 research centers, 10 academic journals, and numerous newsletters, presses, conferences, and associations devoted to promoting and sharing research on women. One goal of many women's studies practitioners is "mainstreaming," meaning that feminist scholarship be incorporated into the entire curriculum, rather than be segregated on the fringe, available to those already interested and committed, or injected almost at random into a traditional syllabus. Other feminists, however, fear that mainstreaming could put women's studies into the hands of faculty members, particularly men, who are not sufficiently knowledgeable of women's issues nor truly comprehending of women's experiences and contributions. Fifty campuses are currently involved in mainstreaming projects through which various means are employed, such as seminars, workshops, and institutes for faculty on scholarship on women, to develop ways to incorporate women's scholarship into disciplines, seminars and colloquia, course materials, and/or all introductory level courses.

This institutionalization of feminist scholarship over the past fifteen years has created a climate in which it can be nurtured and grow, as well as provided it with partial, if not full, legitimacy. Within many disciplines, there is a healthy and energetic school of feminist thought, primarily due to the support women have given each other's work. There is evidence, however, that women's studies have had the most difficulty gaining a foothold at the more prestigious institutions, where academic fashion continues to be set and emulated. Feminist scholars call for the recognition of the androcentrism of traditional research, the denial of the male experience as universal, and the equal valuing of work on and by women. Carl Deglar, a practitioner and champion of feminist scholarship, asks "How can men have their consciousness raised so that they are able to recognize the sex-specific origins and definitions of their fields and thus not dismiss out of hand as irrelevant the concerns that inform as well as motivate the new research by women about women?" (Deglar 1982). Indeed, that question haunts woman scholars in their attempts to gain recognition of their woman-of-knowledge role.

The major issue of this chapter, whether academic women and men play the faculty role in different ways, is indeed an important and complex one. But it is not an impossible issue to deal with. For one thing, the dichotomy is not so great for the majority of faculty, as they are employed at teaching-oriented institutions, and are therefore more likely, whether they are men or women, to spend the bulk of their time in the classroom. Similarly, as the percentage of faculty women with Ph.D.'s and the number of women at top research institutions rise, the number of women in the women-of-knowledge category should rise as well.

But should faculty women strive to be more like faculty men? If faculty women can indeed be characterized by their greater attention to and concern for students, then the question may be raised whether women should attempt to persuade institutions to value those functions, rather than join the competitive, even cut-throat race in which their male colleagues are engaged. This dilemma is often present when women enter traditionally male arenas.

But there are reasons why women should strive to be women-of-knowledge. The first is an issue of equity; women should have the same opportunity as men to develop and use their talents. Another is status, for as long as major institutions such as Harvard, Yale, and Stanford reward faculty for their research, the status hierarchy at other institutions is likely to be based on productivity, at least to some extent. Third, if women do not contribute to scholarship, disciplines will continue to be defined in male-centered ways, both in content and methodology. Women's perspectives and experiences are needed to create a fuller and more accurate body of knowledge about the world. Finally, women are needed to be role models and mentors to aspiring scholars. To deprive male and female students of the experience of seeing women as women-of-knowledge may indeed perpetuate women's relative absence in that role in the future. Thus, the argument that women prefer and are best-suited to be teachers, and therefore that tendency should be accepted and valued, is a shortsighted one, at best.

Although Bernard herself stressed the reciprocal nature of roles, she addressed it from the question of whether women are able to effectively perform certain roles, given the response of others, rather than the ways in which the responses of others have resulted in discriminatory practices. For example, the expectations of others may have led to a situation in which women are judged most appropriate to teach undergraduate courses, or to do tedious committee assignments, or to advise and counsel individual students. Department chairs may feel less compunction asking women to take on additional, yet unrewarded tasks, or undergraduates may feel more comfortable approaching them with personal or academic problems than they would with male faculty members. These expectations may in fact lead to faculty women being placed in positions in which there is less opportunity to do research, as they are not perceived as scholars by others.

Closely related to the issue of role reciprocity is the evaluation of women. The bulk of the research indicates that women are likely to be evaluated more harshly than men, particularly in traditionally male areas. They are seen as having less authority, and their opinions are accepted less readily. This would have an obvious impact on the ability of women to be seen as women-of-knowledge.

The problem may be compounded by the kinds of scholarship women may produce. Bernard saw women's work to be precise, thorough, and noncontroversial. She neglected to see the possibility that this might be the only type of work by women that gets recognition, although she suggested that ground-breaking work by women simply may not be acknowledged as such.

Furthermore, the scholarship of women may be different in style and substance than mainstream academic scholarship, which has tended to focus on the perspectives, accomplishments, and experiences of men. The "gatekeepers" of the academic publishing world—editors and reviewers—are likely to see it as inappropriate for their publications, which may result in it being published primarily in feminist journals and never widely shared. When women do ground-breaking work, particularly with regard to their own experiences, it is likely to be denigrated or ignored. The Freedman tenure case at Stanford, cited earlier, is but one example of institutional reluctance to accept and reward scholarship on women. This is not to suggest that all research and writing done by women is of a feminist nature, but rather that when it is, women may be penalized for it. One reflection of this penalty is that women are less likely to be seen as women-of-knowledge, as their work may lack the visibility and prominence of men's.

Women find themselves in a double bind. When they act in stereotypically female ways by being compliant, cooperative, nurturing, and conscientious, they find themselves locked into tasks and functions which are consistent with those roles, namely teaching and service to students. When they exhibit assertive, vigorous behavior or express challenging, innovative ideas, they may be ostracized and penalized for acting in those ways, and still not given access to the resources of time, funding, equipment, and staff to do research. Either way, they have less opportunity and support to become prominent within their fields or their institutions.

One form of discrimination is having opportunities limited due to the expectations of others. Women may be assigned to or kept in less-desirable roles, simply because they may perform them well and are perceived as being appropriate for them. However, there is a flaw to that logic. One would not keep a promising mathematician at Calculus I level because he or she had done well there. Rather, one would look for other ways to develop and expand those demonstrated abilities. Women, however, are too often kept in limited functions, with their potential unrecognized and unacknowledged. This is not to suggest that research is by definition better than teaching, or that all women strive to be women-of-knowledge, but rather that women may be systematically denied access to that channel of endeavor, which also happens to be better rewarded within the academic status hierarchy.

Thus, women's greater likelihood to be found in the role of teacher can be attributed to a number of varying, yet powerful forces. These factors have an impact, not only on the roles women play and the recognition they receive, but on their aspirations and self-image as well.

There are some indications that the situation has improved since Bernard's time and that it will continue to do so. These include the growing prominence of women's studies and feminist scholarship, the expansion of women's scholarly and professional networks for communication and support, the increasing numbers of women faculty at research institutions, the implementation of anti-discrimination laws, and the increasing publication rates for women. If these phenomena continue and grow, perhaps faculty women will finally have access to the core of intellectual life within the academy, and will receive long overdue recognition for their ideas, perspectives, and contributions to scholarship.

4
Informal Relationships

I had to chuckle, several weeks ago. I'm in the process of a difficulty with salary and there's a tenured faculty person who's helping me with it and both of us are members of the Nautilus Club that's across the street. Several weeks ago—we'd been trying to get in touch with each other and had been missing each other—several weeks ago, we happened to walk into the locker room at the same time and we started talking about the situation and brainstorming what we could do and I said, "We've arrived. Here we are in the locker room, talking about this problem. This is the network—the 'good ole boy' network. We've arrived!" It was just such a chuckle for both of us.

—interview with a faculty woman

A sense of isolation and difference pervades the histories of women of achievement in traditionally male arenas. There are few other women in comparable situations, and while an individual woman may see herself as simply another member of the group, her male colleagues are likely to perceive her as being quite different from themselves. This perception of difference, often coupled with denigrating attitudes if not indeed caused by them, results in women's exclusion from the truly meaningful and important interactions with male colleagues and superiors.

Up to this point, this study examined the lower status of women, as compared to men, on a variety of quantifiable measures of standard academic success; the next two chapters look at the ways in which the informal relationships operate, and the ways in which women cope with their isolation from them.

There are two primary kinds of interactions experienced by faculty women. The first, upon which this chapter will focus, is between

77

academic women and their colleagues, and involves the ways in which they are treated and perceived within their departments, disciplines, and institutions. The second, which the following chapter examines, is the relationship between, on the one hand, female students or junior faculty, and, on the other, senior faculty who are in a position to serve as sponsors or mentors to beginning academics.

Role Anomalies

Jessie Bernard claimed that women's sense of isolation results from the role anomaly caused by their serving in a faculty capacity. She contended that for academic women, sex is the most salient characteristic as a determiner of status. Regardless of the role the faculty woman plays, be it scholar or dean or teacher, she is seen first and foremost as a woman, and secondarily as a woman in a particular role. Thus, men feel more comfortable when women are acting in ways which are consistent with their stereotypical roles within society at large, such as sex object or provider of emotional-expressive functions. In fact, even when women deviate from these roles, men may perceive and treat them as if they acted in accordance with them. Bernard wrote that these role anomalies cause confusion for men, who then have to decide how to respond.

Much of the emphasis of the contemporary women's movement has been on the changing role of women, with regard to their life choices and, by necessity, the responses of those around them. One might expect women in faculty roles to present less of an anomaly than when *Academic Women* was published. Yet the research shows that many of the same responses still occur.

This is confirmed by the work of Rosabeth Moss Kanter, whose landmark book, *Men and Women of the Corporation*, described the situation women face as minorities, 'tokens' in her terminology, within predominantly male work groups. She found the women to be highly visible, to be perceived as being different from the majority group members, and to be seen as representing and demonstrating the stereotypical characteristics of their gender. In turn, these perceptions heighten each woman's isolation and the pressure on her to perform. All her acts grow more visible and carry extra symbolic weight. Any woman may represent all womanhood in stereotypical form—"mother," a provider of service and emotional support; "seductress," an object of attempted or imagined sexual conquest;

"pet," a cheerleader who inspires affection and amusement; and "iron maiden," who does not fall into a stereotypically female role category and is thus viewed and treated with apprehension (Kanter 1977).

There are now more women in academic and professional life, yet as Kanter suggests, this does not mean that the role confusion and expectations imposed on women have been erased. For example, the issue of sexuality is still present in other's perceptions of women, serving either to focus attention on their appearance, sexual availability, or personal life, or to inhibit informal interactions because of a fear of a perceived or real heterosexual involvement. The notion that women are primarily responsible for the care of their families may lead to special allowances in that area, yet coupled with doubts regarding their commitment to their professional lives. Women who do not fit into these stereotyped roles are penalized for that as well, since women who seem to put their work before domestic duties or who seem indifferent to heterosexual attractions are perceived as tough, cold, heartless, or pushy. It is a no-win situation. There is a restricted range of roles within which women can comfortably operate, yet they may be penalized even if their behavior falls within it. When women act in an "appropriate" fashion, they may be treated with chivalry and affection, yet their work may not be taken seriously. Yet, women who act in more stereotypically male ways may find themselves outsiders as well.

William Goode referred to the narrow range of social roles which women are thought to occupy, which he felt was typical of the way in which members of subordinate groups are viewed by the superordinates. He wrote of the confusion these perceptions in turn cause for men:

> Men have found their women difficult to understand for a simple reason: they have continued to think of them as a set of roles (above all else, mothers and wives), but in fact women do not fit these roles, not only not now, but not in the past either . . . At any point, men could observe that women were breaking out of their social roles, and men experienced that as puzzling. However, it is only recently that men have faced the blunt fact that there is no feminine riddle at all: Women are as complex as men are, and always will escape the confinements of any narrow set of roles. [Goode 1982]

In addition to all of the usual pressures faculty members encounter on the job, women experience extra sources of stress. In Kanter's 'skewed' groups, in which men make up at least 85 percent of the membership—which include the majority of college and university departments—women are perceived in a number of ways which affect how they are treated. According to Kanter, 'token' women face dilemmas and contradictions to which members of the male majority are immune. When successful, they are seen as exceptions; when they fail, it is seen as inevitable. Moreover, women are often unaware of these perceptions.

Unfortunately, the kind of blatant and subtle discrimination against women these perceptions result in cannot be addressed with legal or institutional action, even though they are no less real or harmful than out-and-out discrimination. Eileen Shapiro devised a scheme of categories and definitions of nonactionable forms of discrimination to help women faculty recognize, acknowledge, understand, and respond to incidents which occur. These categories include condescension, hostility, "backlashing," role stereotyping, sexual innuendo, and invisibility (Shapiro 1982). Women are singled out, seen as different, and assessed as to whether their behavior conforms to that seen as appropriate for their gender. As tokens, they are seen not only as different, but as inferior and sexual. The "unaware" and "out-of-consciousness" character of the harassment exacerbates the burden experienced by the woman who may doubt her own analysis.

One faculty member described the way in which women tend to be seen as less able than men to carry out important responsibilities.

> The men involved have absolutely no idea that they're discriminating. I mean, they'd be absolutely horrified if you told them that there was a difference in the way they treated women and the way they treated men. You know, "If there's anything really major that has to be taken care of, you better let us handle it." Either the women have to be protected—it's a combination really of protecting them and not really being sure they can handle anything that needs competence.

Others described incidents of hostility. In one account, a faculty woman, who doubles as the wife of a faculty member, described an incident in which three male colleagues "teased" her about her relationship with her husband, implying that he must be "hen-pecked" and suspicious of her relationship with them.

> But these were old-fashioned men, *gentlemen* even. But gentlemen surely wouldn't talk to a lady the way they were talking to me. But I wasn't a lady, was I? If I were, I'd be home cooking dinner. My mind was spinning, trying to understand them, to understand me, to understand why I was losing, when it was they who were afraid. For sud-denly I saw that they *were* afraid and that in their fear, they were forcing on me all the shadowy figures that were crowded into the backs of their minds. Women in power, not in their place, not serving men, not serving them. They weren't worried about my family at all. Or my hus-band. They were worried about themselves. [Stitzel 1982]

In a case at a professional conference, a psychologist described how women were portrayed as sex objects, for the amusement of the predominantly, and assumed to be entirely, male audience.

> I have been at too many professional meetings, where the "joke" slide was a woman's body, dressed or undressed. A woman in a bikini is a favorite with past and perhaps present presidents of psychological associations. The business of making jokes at women's bodies constitutes a primary social-sexual assault. The ensuing raucous laughter expresses the shared understanding of what is assumed to be women's primary function—to which we can always be reduced. Showing pictures of nude and sexy women insults us; it puts us in our place. You may think you are a scientist, it is saying, but what you really are is an object for our pleasure and amusement. Don't forget it. [Weisstein 1977]

Mostly, the women in this study described instances of role ster-eotyping. In one case, a woman was surprised to realize that her sex was an important part of the way in which others saw her, as it was not an important part of the way she described herself as a profes-sional. This is consistent with Kanter's insight on the heightened visibility of tokens with respect to their element of difference, re-gardless of whether the token herself is aware of the process. This woman recalled:

> I remember one instance where I was invited to a dinner
> at the faculty club for something or other and afterwards,
> someone came up to me and said, "I'm sure that so and
> so was very glad when you walked in because until that
> time, she was the only woman in the room." I said, "That
> did not occur to me. I did not observe that, being in that
> situation. There was a bunch of people and I was one of
> them." And he said, "You're kidding. You had to have
> noticed that," and I said, "No, that's not part of my out-
> look on life. I'm not a woman engineer—I'm an engineer."

Other examples of role stereotyping occur when women are expected to exhibit certain types of sex-linked behavior or to fulfill
stereotypically female functions. In one case, the faculty member
was expected to fulfill what Kanter categorized as the mother role,
in that she was expected to carry out mundane tasks in support of
her male colleagues. Of course, this example also illustrates the ease
with which these men expected her to provide clerical assistance,
another stereotypically female function.

> This university was the first place I encountered, or
> maybe became aware of a certain amount of—not sex-
> ism— but a kind of attitude of older male faculty . . . I
> was kind of surprised to work with a committee in which
> it was assumed that I would take notes and then repro-
> duce these notes, and then be scolded if the notes weren't
> reproduced. I was one member of a five person committee
> and I'd never come across that before. There's just some-
> thing subtle that I've experienced here.

In another case, a faculty member reported being placed in the
category of seductress as a way of explaining the attention she received from her renowned faculty mentor; other graduate students
assumed she could never have earned a close relationship on the
basis of her intellect or her work. She was also aware of the presence
of another male/female role stereotype, that of father/daughter.

> When I was in graduate school, I also resented—I had a
> very close relationship with these mentors of mine, a
> couple of whom were men, and one wrote about me in a
> chapter of a book, and I know it had to do with an un-
> conscious—I won't even say sexual fantasy—it wasn't

worked out that way. It had to do with a, you might say, parent also male/female issue . . . But it wasn't anything near overt, and he was as nice to other men as he was to me. In some cases I really resented the fact that men said that I got attention because I was a woman . . . There were a couple of men in the department who wanted his attention also for their work and they didn't get it, and they came up to me and said, "It's because you're a woman. He likes women." I was really angry because I had never appealed to him on that basis.

Another way in which women are affected by role stereotyping is by the parts of their lives that others choose to notice and acknowledge, or ignore and repudiate. Studies show that women have fewer informal conversations with male faculty members about their work than men do (Adler 1976). In this way, a faculty member said that her conversations with some of her male colleagues tended to be about the more comfortable topic, for them, of her motherhood than on her scholarly work.

People come up to me and say, "How's the baby?" and I, wanting to be friendly—I always respond on that level and we get locked into the baby rather than a more private domain, which is "What are you working on?"

Kanter suggests that some women deal with their token status by trying to avoid exhibiting stereotypically feminine characteristics. She also notes that many women, with time, learn to develop a comfortable way of coping with the pressures and problems of being in a token situation. In the following example, this faculty woman described her transition over the years in the clothes she wore.

If anything . . . she [Hennig, in *The Managerial Woman*] makes a point that all of her women that got to be successful, at one time made a decision to start dressing more like women, and when I read that a few years ago, I thought that was nonsense. But in the last few years, I've done exactly that. For instance, all my clothes used to be gray and brown. Now I wear colors . . . I let my nails grow and polish them red, which I never would have dreamed of doing.

Old-Boy Networks

An important component of academic life is the informal network of communication within departments, institutions, and disciplines, which are often the source of important social, political, and intellectual exchange. Being included in them may mean being aware of the latest developments in one's field, having one's work informally critiqued, knowing the latest gossip (the better to negotiate institutional politics), cultivating a research partner, receiving a job reference—all the helpful little opportunities that can add up to a career advantage. Bernard contended that the role confusion felt by men resulted in women being systematically excluded from informal networks by a phenomenon that she labelled the 'stag effect.' This, of course, is better known today as the 'old-boy network.'

What hasn't changed is that these informal relationships are still lacking for today's women scholars. In a survey of more than 1000 faculty women, women cited a feeling of isolation and a desire for networks and support groups as their second highest professional concern. This was particularly true for women in their twenties (27 percent) at the start of their careers (Spencer and Bradford 1982).

The exclusion of women from informal male networks is consistent with Kanter's findings on the treatment of token women in skewed groups. According to Kanter, the presence of a small number of women in a predominantly male work group is seen as a threat by the males, who fear that women, as outsiders, will assess, challenge, and/or change their culture. These feelings can lead to boundary-heightening behavior on the part of men, which results in the exclusion of women from the benefits of group membership.

Eighteen of the twenty women interviewed for this study felt excluded at least to some extent from the old-boy network. They described not being invited to lunch, drinks, athletic activities, general gossiping, or other social activities; not being included in intellectual discussions or invited to collaborate on research projects; or not being invited to join professional associations. It is interesting to note that of those two who did not feel excluded, one is in a virtually all-male field, engineering, and the other is in a virtually all-female field, nursing. Of the others, several had difficulty deciding whether the determining factor was their sex or their race, research interests, foreign birth, leftist politics, or personal characteristics and behavior, including their own lack of initiative in pursuing these contacts. This illustrates the difficulty of assessing informal relationships, as there is a tendency to see them in strictly personal, rather than institutional, terms.

One study of informal networks showed that both male and female faculty members tended to have more colleague/friends of the same sex. This was particularly true of unmarried women, who suffer more than married women for their perceived "deviance." The author speculated that this occurs because single women have assumed professional roles and seem to have rejected conventional ones, and because they do not carry the "protective status" of being married (Kaufman 1978). At the assistant professor rank, men (66.7 percent) were more likely than women (40 percent) to have higher ranked colleague/friends. These findings suggest that, since people tend to stay within their sex in forming friendships, as long as female faculty are less numerous and less likely to be in positions of power, men tend to gain more from their friendships with each other, both in the breadth of their network and the potential for sponsorship.

One of the most harmful effects of the exclusion of females from male networks is on their scholarly work and research productivity. Lionel Lewis (1975) stated:

> It is almost a truism to state that those who do not have a number of students, colleagues, or mentors to call new ideas to their attention, those who are not consulted for advice and information, those who are not in correspondence with those who have friends in high or important places who might help them advance their careers are not in the best position to know what's going on in their field. And as far as such factors are concerned, women are in a more disadvantaged position than men . . . for most, productivity is a function of one's position in the communication system in a discipline.

One study showed that in sociology, women were more likely than men to publish alone, although there has been a significant increase in male/female collaboration from 1967 to 1973 (Mackie 1977).

There is also evidence to suggest that men collaborate differently with women than with men. Another study examined authorship and acknowledgments in 100 randomly selected books in educational psychology. In the four books written by women, there were no acknowledgments. Of those written by men, 75 percent cited other men for intellectual influence, 21 percent cited both men and women, and 5 percent cited only women. For those men acknowledging editorial assistance, about a third cited other men, a third women, and a third both. All 21 books which mentioned clerical services cited women. In all eleven cases in which social support was acknowledged, men cited their wives. In fact, 19 authors in all mentioned their wives—six for intellectual influence, six for editorial assistance, six for clerical services, and eleven for emotional support (Lewis-Beck 1980). These findings suggest that when men work with women, they tend to utilize them, or perhaps to only recognize and acknowledge them, in traditionally feminine roles such as clerical and emotional support. The absence of women from the role of co-author or intellectual influence indicates that men do not involve them in their own research, and, as men make up the bulk of those doing research, that omission is considerable.

One faculty woman interviewed for this study described the way in which women's exclusion from informal relationships has an impact on their scholarship.

> Well, I think the most difficult problem facing women in academics is not getting jobs commensurate with their credentials. I mean, that was the central problem 10 or 15 years ago—I don't think that's the problem so much anymore. I think it's the opportunity that differs now; because so much of what goes on in academics is subjective. So much is access to discussing a project over a drink and then going on to work on a paper together and that kind of camaraderie that generates research interest and brings an entering assistant professor into understanding research, and active participation is often closed to women. It used to be closed because no one thought women would be serious contributors to research, but now I sense that people are concerned about the gossip that might go on if they're working with a female collaborator, particularly a young, new assistant professor.
>
> And then there's the fact that a lot of men just don't feel as comfortable talking over research with a woman as with a man, and these are the same people who, I think, would treat a male and a female with the same record equitably in terms of promotion and in terms of giving them a job. It's just that once they're here—they don't

get the same access. It's not a knowing kind of discrimination—I think it's just the way friendships form.

However, one black faculty woman chose to work alone, fearing that she would be denied credit for her work if she collaborated with others.

> When I started out writing, everything I did in the beginning was by myself. I was a loner, single author, and I did that for a number of reasons. First of all, I wanted to see if I could do it. I needed to validate that and I did get that validated. And the second part—I don't know if this is tied to being a black female—is that sometimes, when you do things in pairs, people don't really think you've done it. I don't know if that's related to blackness or what. So the idea was to establish a name for myself early on— to do it, to try it, to get the feedback. And now I'm at the stage where I'm ready to do it within the context of a research team.

There is a tangible deficit in women's working lives caused by their exclusion from collaboration with men. This is further complicated by the possibility that when they do work with men, their contributions are unseen and unacknowledged, their ideas are credited to others, and that they must cautiously avoid being involved in a potentially exploitative relationship. Nonetheless, women's careers would certainly be enhanced by access to collaboration with the same range and numbers of colleagues as their male counterparts.

Power and Influence

Another aspect of informal relationships is their effect on the influence one has within the department and institution. This is true within any work group, but in academia, where a collegial rather than a hierarchical model governs decision-making, one's informal power is of special importance.

Not surprisingly, the research shows that women have less power and influence within their departments than men. One indication of this is their lesser likelihood of taking an active role in meetings. In a study of assistant professors at a large university, 7 percent of the men and 46 percent of the women reported speaking seldom at departmental meetings, while 43 percent of the men and 15 percent of the women spoke often (Glenwick et al. 1978). This is consistent with Kanter's hypotheses that people low in organizational power tend to be "less talkative in meetings with high power people," and that people whose type is represented in small proportion would "try to become 'socially invisible,' not to stand out so much."

A study of 321 faculty members at public community colleges found that, compared to men, women had significantly less perceived participation in decision-making, job involvement, and job satisfaction, and had more job-related tension. The women reported having less influence over their job situation, greater difficulty getting their ideas across to superiors, and feeling less influential in their superiors' decisions and less frequently consulted. They also reported frequently being unable to obtain job-related information from others (Hallon and Gemmill 1976). These findings suggest that women are less likely to be part of and to benefit from informal networks of influence and information, which would inevitably lead to lower satisfaction at work.

Half of the women interviewed for this study reported feeling satisfied with the influence they had within their departments. Several of them felt their satisfaction was due to special circumstances of some kind, such as having an important committee assignment or being in a predominantly female department.

Of the women who did not feel satisfied, some felt it was due to their own lack of initiative in pursuing a position of influence.

> No, not at all [have enough influence]. I behave in a very reticent way. I've never spoken at a departmental meeting. No, I don't deserve it because I never sought it out. I mean, I got my Ph.D. very young and I started looking when I was 26 and I felt like I was a kid and sort of out of place.

> I'm excluded a little here. But I don't care. Again, my long term goal isn't to get tenure here and sit at my desk and be a researcher forever . . . I also look at that as in my control. If I wanted to be included more I know exactly who I could go to. I could start playing tennis instead of squash—I'm a squash player—they all play tennis here. If I wanted to change that, I could have tennis partners

One of the consequences of being excluded from the old-boy network is not having its support in the larger university community. For academics, contacts within the entire faculty can be useful when decisions regarding budget, tenure, promotion, or academic policy are being made. One faculty woman described the impact her exclusion from male networks had on her fight for tenure.

> I do think it took a battle for me to get tenure, not through my department, but at the university level. And I do think that had I been a male, that wouldn't have happened. Again, not any overt discrimination, but I think I would have had some men in the department who would have felt a strong personal loyalty to getting me tenure—who would have argued immediately and vociferously and I would have gotten tenure immediately to quiet that argument down, rather than ultimately everybody supporting me, but not loudly and vociferously.

Thus, exclusion from male networks results in a number of disadvantages for women. They have fewer opportunities to work collaboratively on research projects. They are less likely to be informed of the latest developments in their fields and to benefit from informal discussion of their ideas and their work. They are less likely to receive career advice and assistance, and have to "learn the ropes" the hard way. They have fewer political allies to lobby for them or their ideas. They have less influence within their departments and have a harder time being heard by their colleagues. Additionally, women are deprived of a sense of community in their work environment and may feel isolated and unsupported. Obviously, enduring even a few of these hardships puts women at a disadvantage.

Women's Networks

Recently, however, female associations often referred to as "old-girl networks" have formed within various professions, and particularly within academia. These networks serve a number of functions—promoting scholarly sharing, providing professional assistance, increasing political clout, providing emotional and social support. They range from national associations such as the American Association of University Women, to professional development and career assistance organizations such as the Higher Education Resource Service (HERS) or the American Council on Education-National Identification Program (ACENIP), to discipline-centered groups such as the Society for Women in Philosophy or the Modern Language Association Commission on the Status of Women, to campus-based political or social organizations, to informal networks and alliances.

There are some who would claim that seeking out other women is self-defeating. They would argue that women should instead try to infiltrate and join the male networks, where currently the power resides. Some believe that to be associated with other women is harmful; women's affiliations may be viewed as suspicious, second-class or subversive. One of the faculty members interviewed seemed to share that view, for when she was asked whether she sought out other women at P_____, she replied, "No. I wouldn't want to be identified as one of the 'woman professors.' "

Yet, if Kanter's conception of tokens within skewed groups is correct, women will never be able to participate fully in those relationships if their representation continues to be low. Even with equal representation, there is evidence that men tend to exclude women and seek out other men to conduct formal and informal business. It seems clear that women need to turn to other women, if only to decrease their isolation and build a power base. The founders of Women for Equal Opportunity at the University of Pennsylvania, an organization which has provided political and legal support for women, wrote:

> We argue that we need a separate network now more than ever, in view of rising expectations still largely unmet; that psychological support may mean at least as much as initial qualifications in giving women the courage to try and the will to succeed; and that women's work not only is not done, but may never be done. In short, it is quite possible that, before significant numbers of women can enter the male network on anything like equal terms, we shall need a network of our own that will intersect with a male network without losing its own identity or compromising its goals. [Childers et al. 1981]

Most of the women who were interviewed were enthusiastic about their alliances with other women.

Well, feminists say, and this is true, we have an old girl network. One reason that at least feminists in literature have done very well and sort of gotten very established positions is that some of us—many of us— we organized very early, and we networked. I mean, it isn't entirely true to say we copied men; we took the most powerful part of that . . . I could not have survived without my women friends and colleagues and networks.

I would say that a lot of my progress is due to simultaneity with many of my friends and colleagues. We're very aware of helping each other out and keeping each other informed, recommending each other for positions that come up, and helping each other's students whenever we can.

The existence of female networks does not mean that all women within them have identical concerns and points of view. In fact, one faculty woman felt that the differences among women were a sign of strength, rather than of divisiveness, as is sometimes charged.

And there's a tremendous divergence among the women. And I think that for me it is very disappointing when it doesn't occur and it's exhilarating when it does. Fortunately, there are already—even though there aren't enough—there are enough women around that the community can tolerate a certain amount of subtlety. It's not a "woman right or wrong" kind of support, even though there are differences between what you can say in private in those women's groups and what you say in public.

For some of the women in this study, the networks within their disciplines were most important.

I'm involved in the women's caucus of the American Public Health Association, which is concerned with women in health care. So I'm attempting to broaden that network on a grassroots and national level. And the response is real positive. Always. "More!" "Join our ranks!" "That's great!" And it's nice—it's a nice feeling and there's a nice sense of sisterhood.

And in my own field of economics, there's very much an old girl's network, too, with respect to the women that are fairly prominent in the field. It in fact was very important to me. By coming here, they took notice of me, I mean I got notice of the old girl network. They didn't get me my job, but after I got here they sort of kept track of women at the major institutions, and they immediately took me in and as a result, I knew women at all the prominent institutions, including very senior women. And that has been very important because that has gotten me more access to professional things than any of my male mentors.

There are some very fine women who are in Latin American studies with whom I've come in contact and who I like very much. Part of it is affinity and part of it is they seem to have more energy and "go" than some of the men I've worked with.

One of the faculty members felt that her career had clearly and directly benefited from her feminist scholarship and access to feminist networks.

I was lucky. I was here at a good time. Also, being a feminist critic, and this I didn't do on purpose. I mean, this is just what I write and what I teach—it's me. We have a network and we have an identity within English, so that my work and my books have gotten a hearing that they wouldn't have had if I were a man and wrote the same kind of thing ... If someone wants a feminist speaker, you know—some university or symposium, they'll get me or somebody else. It gives me an identity beyond the private that was sheer luck.

Many of the other women noted the existence of a network within the university.

I think that at P_____, the old girl network is stronger than the old boy network, internal to campus. The reason that is so is that the women know each other better than the men know each other. Now, the men, however, have more power, so having a weaker network, they can control more because they have more power to start out with. But the women definitely make better use of whatever power mechanisms they have.

Several of the women in fact talked about the unspoken support they felt from other women within the institution, even if they were not in personal or professional contact. Just knowing that the women were there made them feel less isolated and vulnerable.

> In point of fact, there is a very strong network of women who I feel comfortable I can call. They're sort of the invisible hand and eye looking over my career.

> The thing that I'm most happy about is that there is now a group of women on campus to whom one can relate and you don't have the feeling of being all alone in a university like P_____, which is still a really male institution—incredibly so. And you can have a problem and mention it to a couple of people and you get help without even asking. There are people there that you can turn to and that just didn't used to be the case.

> I have the fortune of having a colleague with whom I'm not very close, but there is a woman in my department who is a feminist and who is very good, and she's a tough cookie and she's run interference, I think, for me. I mean, we've never discussed it, but I do feel that in a way she's cleared the way for me.

Despite the growth of these networks, however, not all women have felt the same welcome, support, and compatibility within them. Minority women, by race, ethnicity, sexual orientation, or disability have often felt a double isolation—from mainstream, male relationships and from white female networks, as well. One black faculty member stated:

> I've been here since September 1969 . . . I never have and I never will be part of the inner circle and I've always recognized that. Nor do I have a need to . . . I recognize how strong the old ties are that go back 10 years, maybe 15 years—such is life.

In an essay about her experience in academia, one black lesbian made a plea for support from colleagues, illustrating the critical need for connection, both personal and political.

What would help me is this: That those of us who are Black lesbians in academia at least would start a survival and support network—newsletter, once-a-month chain letter, union, whatever, so we won't feel so alone and isolated. In other words, establish some sort of system for mutual survival and *celebration*. A system to prevent our being individually devastated and individually negated. [Davenport 1982]

Given the very small numbers of minority women on any campus, it can be difficult for these women to seek each other out, and when they do, they may find they have little in common besides their race and gender. Another black woman stated:

It's tough. We always tend to want to network with people like ourselves, but there are not many people around like me. There are only four black women. I don't have anything in common with them except we're all faculty members. So we stay off in our own schools.

Even separate from issues of difference, all women do not relate to other women in the same way. Based on her study of 42 academic women at five universities, Katherine Jensen contended that there were three modal categories of academic women with regard to the integration of academic culture and women's culture. The first group, designated as "normative reoriented," aimed towards the male career model. These women saw a clear distinction between their personal and professional lives, and tended to give attention to work over personal issues. They claimed no female role models and no affiliations with other women. The second group, whom she designated as the "value reaffirmed," attempted to experience the "best of both worlds," combining traditional feminine and academic cultural expectations. They assumed a male orientation towards their work, except for the added responsibility of home and family, for which they expected no special treatment from their institutions. They saw themselves as models to female students and sought out female faculty, but their important relationships were with men. The third group, the "career reconstituted," consisted of women who called themselves feminists, saw themselves as female role models, belonged to women's networks, and worked towards an integration of the personal and professional in their work.

The women interviewed for this study did not fit neatly into these categories, although much of what they said was consistent with Jensen's categorizations. For example, the two women in a virtually male-exclusive field came closest to the normative reoriented model. With respect to relationships with other women, one said:

> It's interesting because I view things as quite homogeneous—everyone is a male. I have to mention that when I was in Minnesota, there was a women who was visiting me, and I found it to be quite a unique situation—sort of like there was somewhat of a friendship that was, in a sense, different. And I always wondered, what if I was in a field with this many women around, and does one's interactions with one's colleagues—is it anything different? I can't tell you that. I've always been around a lot of men.

Several of the women fit most closely into the value reaffirmed category. These women were represented within various categories of age, rank, and marital status. It is interesting that this group was the most likely to see academia as a meritocracy, in which the truly worthy and hardworking could succeed. In speaking of her own success, one woman said:

> But then, [my success is] because of me. Margaret Mead way back then didn't have any problems either. There have always been women, I think, who have always been smart enough and perceptive enough who don't encounter these problems ... I'm all in favor of E.R.A. and all that business, because even though I can do it without it, most people can't do it without it. It's not just women, it's men also—most men couldn't do it in that position without legal backup.

Another said:

> I think that women will do just fine if they're prepared. You know it's hard in some areas and you have to recognize that it's going to be hard in some areas because there are male chauvinists, but I think that if you're really competent, then you can succeed.

Most of the women fell into the career reconstituted category, in that they sought new ways to define and combine their personal, professional, and intellectual lives—by doing research on woman-related topics, forming alliances with female colleagues and students, becoming involved with women's concerns on campus, and playing a nontraditional role with respect to marriage and family.

Identification with Feminism

Also significant is the way women define themselves with respect to feminism. Admittedly, there is dispute as to the meaning of that term. However, one can generally assume that feminism means a belief in the equality of women and men, a sense that women are oppressed in today's society, support for women's rights, and a commitment to act in ways which are consistent with these values.

One might guess that women who have achieved a certain level of professional success, particularly in a nontraditional arena, would automatically see themselves as feminists. However, this was not true of the 20 women interviewed for this study, despite remarkably similar lives in terms of career success, intellectual achievement, and nontraditional family arrangements. In response to the question, "Would you call yourself a feminist?" only nine responded positively, without qualifications.

Eight of the women responded somewhat positively, but expressed some reservations or ambivalence. For example, several felt unsure of the definition. Others pointed out that they were not fighters or politically active. Another felt that describing herself as such would penalize her with her male colleagues, saying, "I'm a feminist, but I'm not going to wear a sign and let these guys down the hall see it, because that's going to make them run in the opposite direction." Others felt they had not earned the label, although they acknowledged that others may see them as such. For example, one woman said, "I've always been involved in those kinds of activities [women's], but I don't have the legitimacy to call myself a feminist." Another stated, "I'm hoping I'm a feminist. I'm trying to learn what I need to know to become one."

Of the three women who were certain that they weren't feminists, one seemed to be leaning somewhat in that direction, in saying, "The more I experience certain types of behavior, the more I'm sympathetic to certain things." The other two were openly hostile to the idea; one said, "I don't have time to worry about picayune things."

The conversations with these women seem to suggest that there is little relationship between one's level of achievement, behavior, interests, or life circumstances and one's self-definition. All of the women were able to analyze and describe the impact—often negative—of their gender on their experiences and careers. Yet, not all were willing to place these experiences within a larger cultural or institutional context of sexism, nor to incorporate an added political dimension into their self-definition, even taking into account differences in the definition of the term feminism. It would be interesting to investigate the turning points, if indeed they exist, experienced by about half of the women which enabled them unqualifiedly to describe themselves as feminists.

This is an interesting issue for investigation within any category or professional group of women. However, it is further compounded by academia's particular nature—in the generation of knowledge and in the training of others. The extent to which women professors see themselves as feminists could have implications for both functions.

Part of seeing one's world from a feminist perspective is recognizing the institutionalization of sexism and its direct and indirect impact on the lives of women. This sexism is as much a part of the subtle processes of forming exclusionary working and personal relationships as of more blatant and quantifiable forms of discrimination.

There is real reluctance on the part of many, however, to term these patterns sexism. Men may simply feel that they like certain men better than certain women, attributing this to personality compatibility or common interests, or perceived unappealing characteristics in the women. Women may blame themselves for their exclusion. This was true of several of the women interviewed for this study, who felt that if they changed their behavior in some way, such as being more assertive in meetings or playing tennis instead of squash, they would be included in the old boy network to a greater extent. While they may be right to some degree, the fact remains that women are, as a group, more likely than men to be excluded, regardless of their individual behavior or characteristics. As a result, the conclusion cannot be escaped that exclusion is a form of sex discrimination.

Unfortunately, it is a difficult one to address. People are not likely to perceive their choice of lunch or tennis companions as a sexist act. Moreover, it is not only impossible but undesirable to dictate who may associate with whom. Still, because the outcome is such that women are systematically denied access to the benefits of these relationships, the importance and meaning of these choices should not be underestimated, nor should they be seen as outside the realm of institutional responsibility and action.

It has been suggested by Bernard, Kanter, and others that one of the causes of women's exclusion has been the discomfort and confusion men feel at the anomaly of a woman in a faculty role. Men tend to perceive women within certain narrow and limited social roles, as William Goode suggests in his essay, "Why Men Resist." When they step outside of these roles, men respond by retreating to the male group, with which they feel comfortable.

Again, there exists a double-bind for women. "Feminine" behavior casts them in restrictive roles which can lead to their exclusion from equal participation in informal relationships; "masculine" behavior may lead to their being ostracized and disdained by men. According to Kanter, this situation will persist until the number of women within departments and institutions increases to a more balanced level. While greater numerical equality undoubtedly would be helpful, the real issue is equality of power. Men make up only half of the population of the world, but they are still the superordinate group.

One small but important step towards changing the balance of power in academia has been the emergence of women's networks. In addition to their concrete benefits, these networks illustrate the shift away from the centrality of men which Goode describes. They are not merely a reaction and a second-best alternative to women's exclusion from male networks, but rather speak to the positive valuing by women of each other's work, experience, and support. In fact there are some who would argue that these networks constitute the most vital development within the recent history of American higher education, and that this shift in centrality has opened institutions and disciplines to new and exciting dimensions in scholarship, curriculum, methodology, and practice.

Nonetheless, women clearly see the necessity of inclusion in informal relationships with men, so as to be full participants in academic life and full recipients of its benefits. While there has been progress over the past two decades, women faculty continue to be excluded, which in turn affects all facets of their career satisfaction and success. As the number of women in academia increases, there will almost necessarily be an accompanying increase in informal interaction between men and women, which should help break down myths, stereotypes, and barriers. At the same time, men's attitudes and behavior must change in such a way that they come to value and seek out more heterogeneous and inclusive networks. For such a shift to occur, the problem must be addressed institutionally on all levels—by mandates, rewards and example from academic and administrative leadership; by standards of representation set and enforced by associations and governing councils; by genuine efforts for female authorship by publishers and journal editors; by political alliances and lobbies formed by like-minded male and female colleagues; and by confrontation by men and women of actions and attitudes which serve to keep women isolated and invisible. It will only be then that women will truly have access to the same institutional support as men, and that academia will be enriched by the benefit of women's fullest participation.

5
Sponsors and Protégés

I would have been so happy to have a professor like me . . . I'm
this person, and I have tenure and they know that, and I'm doing
it and I love my work and I hope in that sense that I am [a role
model]. I don't want them to turn into me.

—interview with a faculty woman

I know that I am [a role model]. I am because when minority
students get into trouble, they'll come talk to me. It's extra
work that no one ever acknowledges. No credit's ever given for
that . . . I don't have to do outreach. I'm the only black woman
here.

—interview with a faculty woman

The sponsor/protégé (or mentor/protégé) relationship has long been
considered an important one in the academic world. The sponsor
may serve many functions for the protégé. First, the sponsor intro-
duces and initiates the protégé in the customs, demands, and expectations of academic life. Second, the sponsor shares his or her
wisdom and knowledge with the protégé, and provides encouragement and comments on his or her work. Third, the sponsor can
provide career assistance for the protégé by making recommenda-
tions to his or her colleagues at other institutions, or simply by
sharing a bit of the deflected glow from his or her own shining
reputation. Perhaps most important, the sponsor helps to form
within the protégé the sense of him or herself as a member of the
profession, encouraging and fostering a self-image as a legitimate
member of the community of scholars. For the sponsor comes the
satisfaction of initiating new talent into her or his profession, and

101

the gratification of being admired, imitated, and sought out for advice, assistance, and inspiration.

The encouragement of a sponsor may be particularly important for women, whose sense of entitlement and belonging within their profession may be somewhat shakier than their male counterparts'. Although some have questioned whether sufficient evidence exists to prove the necessity of having a sponsor for career success, and while there is little quantitative proof of its actual impact (Speizer 1981), the popular notion prevails, based primarily on observational and anecdotal evidence, that having a sponsor is a decided and perhaps critical advantage, particularly at the start of an academic career.

Sponsorship of Women

According to interviews with college and university administrators, seven primary elements constitute an effective protégé/sponsor relationship—offering accessible and frequent interaction, providing opportunities for visibility, giving feedback on both strengths and weaknesses, receiving institutional recognition for sponsors, making allowances for failure, being open to sponsoring a diversity of students, and making a genuine commitment to one's protégé (Moore 1982).

For example, an extensive survey of graduate students at 25 institutions shows that the single best predictor of the perceived quality of the graduate department climate is the nature and quality of the student-faculty relations, including accessibility and whether the faculty treated the students with respect. A further analysis of the data showed a positive relationship between the number of female faculty and the rating of the environment for learning by women students (Hartnett 1976).

Relationships with faculty can also have an influence on the career aspirations of graduate students. Feldman found that women who had close relationships with faculty were more likely to have more ambitious academic career plans. He speculated that this was because they would be likely to have a more professional self-image, and better help in obtaining jobs.

Yet women are more likely than men to be excluded from this sort of relationship with senior faculty. A number of reasons have been suggested for this exclusion. The vast majority of senior faculty members are men and faculty men may see women as being different from themselves, less intellectually able, less committed and dedicated, or simply inappropriate for academic careers. As Kanter suggested, they may be unable to envision a woman outside of traditional supportive roles, least of all as a potential full-fledged colleague and contributor to the body of work of their discipline. As a result, they may be particularly concerned about the possibility or appearance of a heterosexual relationship. Such feelings would obviously color their interactions with women and make them less likely and willing to devote energy and time to women's development and careers.

This differential treatment can lead to a number of major and minor advantages given to male students. If male students are more likely to be asked to collaborate with senior faculty in research or the writing of a paper, if they are given more opportunities to showcase their work, if they are more likely to be engaged in discussion of their work or the latest developments in their fields, if they are more likely to meet informally other scholars in their own and related disciplines, then they have received a distinct advantage. This exclusion may be even more likely to occur with women perceived to be even further away from the "mainstream," such as minority women, disabled women, older women, or lesbians (Hall and Sandler 1983).

As more women work their way into the upper faculty ranks, there will be more women available to provide sponsorship to aspiring scholars, particularly to women. Some studies have begun to investigate the impact of the sponsor's gender on the quality and outcome of the relationship. One found that women sponsors were more likely than men to be involved with their students' personal concerns, even though they maintained contact with protégés for shorter periods of time than men. In addition, they were less likely than men to initiate sponsorship relationships with students, and seemed to feel less comfortable with the notion of having a strong influence on another's work or future plans. The authors suggest that this demonstrates a greater tendency for a stronger personal component to the relationships of women, yet the lesser likelihood of relationships being professionally productive. They contend that men seem better able to maintain these linkages, although perhaps less meaningfully, to continue to reap professional benefits for both themselves and their protégés. The study also found that the protégés of men (75 percent) were more likely to stay within academia than the protégés of women (13 percent) (Mokros et al. 1981). This may be a result of the greater professional orientation of male sponsorship, with males seeking out protégés who are likely to remain and succeed within their own field, and women serving as more generalized advisors, supporters, and role models; or also to the lesser success women sponsors may have than their male counterparts in actually paving the way for protégés interested in academic careers. One wonders, however, to what extent this phenomenon is based on choices made by the women sponsors themselves, or is a result of the way in which they are perceived, needed, and utilized by their protégés.

Women faculty are not the only ones eager and willing to sponsor women, and one must not overlook male faculty who do so. One study showed that those men who did have female protégés tended to sponsor a disproportionate number of women, suggesting that there may be particular men who are able to see the potential and worth within women students and who are willing to contribute to their careers (Blackburn et al. 1981). In addition, as more women move into and up the faculty ranks, there may simply be greater numbers of faculty available to act in a mentor role to women. This is particularly significant for minority women, who have been vastly underrepresented on college and university faculties and thus unable to serve as mentors and role models to students. The increase in mentoring opportunities for women may be even further supported as the value of mentoring receives much attention, and thus becomes a more deliberate and widespread practice.

Of the twenty women interviewed for this study, eighteen reported having mentors. Their mentorship occurred in both undergraduate and graduate school, and was provided by faculty members or by graduate students who were farther advanced in their programs.

For one woman, having female faculty mentors encouraged her in choosing a predominantly male field, because they made her less conscious of its "maleness."

> I would say, as an undergraduate, maybe the thing that was most responsible for my going into economics is that the department I was in had about ten faculty and two were women, which relative to other departments in the university, was a fairly good representation of women and so I did not know at that time that economics was an

extremely male field. In fact, the two women were the best people in the department and certainly I took their courses and enjoyed those courses and I guess in some sense was motivated to think about economics through them, because in math I didn't have any similar kinds of mentors . . . Even [though there were] not high percentages, they were women I liked and could identify with. And as long as there are women whom you like and can appreciate as role models, I had less of a sense of being in a field that I was isolated in. I think if those same numbers had been women I didn't like, I would have felt more isolated.

For some of the women, however, having a female mentor was an impossibility, simply because senior women were virtually nonexistent in their fields.

Right now around the country, to my knowledge there might be two women with tenure in chemical engineering departments. Now that doesn't mean there are no women in the pipeline, so I see myself in a sense as a cutting edge. . . . So from that sense of having a female mentor, that didn't exist at all.

Ten of the twenty faculty women identified males as their mentors, and reported related advantages. In the following case, the faculty member felt that her male mentor was better able than a woman would have been to negotiate for his female students within the male system.

The fortunate factor in my personal history was that I did have an advisor who was quite exceptional—who was younger and without any kind of ideological commitment to women's lib or anything like that, on an individual personal basis, really went out of his way to work with his graduate students, and given that we were in literature, which is a primarily female field, it was extremely important to have someone like that who could be the liaison between the establishment and the graduate students.

In another case, the faculty women felt that, although her female mentor provided more personal attention, encouragement, and support, her male mentors ultimately did more for her career, as their reputations and connections carried more weight on her behalf.

She helped me probably more than them because it was a very personal involvement and she's a mentor to me, but because she hasn't produced what they have, not in the same way. She is probably somebody I love and respect more than them—they're three very important people in graduate school, two men and a woman—and she's probably the most important in my life and she's also not able to help me as much now professionally because her name doesn't mean the same as theirs.

Role Models

The effectiveness of the role model function has not been proven. One author stated:

There is something intuitively appealing about the concept of role models; it seems plausible that they should have some influence on career selection, and furthermore, it may even be somewhat logical to expect people of "like" kind to have more influence on each other (especially given probabilities of proximity) than people who are "unlike." But we must be honest enough to recognize that all of this lies on a hypothetical, or conjectural plane. The danger lies in elevating the hypotheses into facts before their time, because it is often the case that once elevated, appealing conceptions are resilient against counterfactual evidence. [Cole 1979]

As Cole says, the concept does make intuitive sense. First, women professors can serve as examples of success, and of the appropriateness of women within their disciplines and within academia. Second, they can serve as examples of women who have devoted a substantial amount of energy, effort, and ability towards reaching hard-to-attain goals. Third, they can be seen as women who have chosen relatively nontraditional paths, and can serve as examples of the way in which they've reconciled that choice with other life choices. Finally, they can serve as models in all the ways faculty men do. It seems reasonable to assume that having women perform all of the above would provide encouragement and inspiration to young female observers, particularly those aspiring to nontraditional roles.

One of the best-known studies of the possible effect of role modeling was done by Elizabeth Tidball, who analyzed a two percent sample, taken from *Who's Who of American Women, 1966-71*, of all women "achievers" who had graduated from college over a five-decade period. Graduates of women's colleges were more than twice as likely to be listed as those of coeducational schools. Most important, for each decade, as well as for the entire fifty-year period, the correlation between the number of female faculty and the number of female achievers was highly significant, leading Tidball to conclude, "Women teachers as role models for women students are thus a critical ingredient of a college environment that turns out talented women" (Tidball 1975). Indeed, in another study, male and female Ph.D.'s with advisors of the same sex had more publications four years after graduation that those in cross-sex conditions, suggesting the importance of observing the success and receiving the support of same-sex models (Goldstein 1979).

A great deal of anecdotal evidence confirms the importance of female faculty as role models to female students. Of the women interviewed for this study, virtually all of them saw themselves as role models. Some played that role consciously and deliberately; others saw themselves as such only because others told them that they were. Some examples of the latter case are as follows:

> I think they see me as a role model. Some of them do. It took me a long time to be able to detect signs of it, but I think I have been and am a role model for them. I remember some comments, many, many years ago, around 1968, the women students telling me, "You are someone I would like to emulate," so I suppose that is being a role model.

> Since you asked the question, one student who I had really not worked with at all, who put me in the acknowledgments in the introduction of her dissertation—the fact that I was a role model—even though she was working on another topic and we hadn't worked together at all. So I guess that probably I was for a while, as I said, I don't think it's as crucial anymore because there are more [women faculty].

I have been told in various situations with the different things I have done that perhaps I am, but I don't think of it. I guess because I don't see myself as a female role model. I see myself as a coper.

For others, their sense of themselves as role models stemmed not so much from their own individual achievements but from the fact that there were so few women for students to emulate.

I know I am [a role model]. I know they see me like that—especially here at P_____. Some of them have said to me that I'm the only woman professor they've had here at P_____.

Sure, in lots of ways—positive and negative, I guess. Well, I remember when I first started teaching an evening course in economics and one woman coming up to me and saying—I guess she was the only woman in the class and there were not many woman instructors in those days—saying how absolutely marvelous she felt in the class because I was there, and that was very good. It was very reassuring to me because I was very nervous.

The image projected of the experience of women in academia is not always a positive one, nor should it be.

In fact, one of the most depressing things—when I was here a few years, one of the first women to get a Ph.D. from this department, in fact, went into consulting and didn't go into an academic career and as she left she told me the reason she didn't go into academics is that she could not see herself working as I did for the little bit of reward I got and that depressed me, because it was my experience that led her away from teaching.

When you talked about being a role model, I think one of the most important missions is to be honest and to counter the image that you can present when you get up there and seem terribly self-assured and in control of the situation and having the students realize that beyond that facade is a very insecure, neurotic, anxious individual try ng to cope with too many things at once. It's been very important . . . to have that kind of personal contact—

"It's been really difficult, these have been the consequences; you are not neurotic; and you can get over this.
Basically if you've made it this far it's because you're
pretty solid and better times are ahead."

For others, acting as a positive role model was a part of their job of
which they are highly aware.

When I have the energy, I feel that it is really important
for me, to the extent that I can, to be a positive role model.
I don't want to be a screaming feminist at them, because
then that's all they see, but I want to be a competent,
capable, secure and calm health provider who also happens to be a woman. I hope, in my fantasies, that that's
going to make a difference somewhere down the line—
that that's going to erase 25 years of socialization in another way.

I guess you were probably not at the opening exercises
for freshmen this year. I was because I am chair-elect to
the Senate, and it was the first time I was at them, I guess.
I sat on a platform, along with many other women faculty,
and we heard a whole batch of speakers— the President
and the Provost and the Acting Vice Provost for University Life, a chaplain, a rabbi—all male, an all-male program and the glee club sang—that's also all-male. They
mentioned that 43 percent of the students coming were
female, and looking at the audience they were all female,
and then here were all these men standing up there talking. We made a point of hanging around afterwards, in
academic costumes so we would be recognized as faculty,
talking to students. And many women students came up
to us and said they were so glad to see there were women
faculty. They had certainly never said, but what was
clearly said—was that this was a male institution.

In sum, the women faculty interviewed for this study felt that
serving as a role model was a real and important component of their
jobs. Even those who were not conscious and deliberate in their
efforts did recognize that they served this function in the eyes of
others.

Institutional Action

Since sponsorship helps the initiation of young scholars, it seems clear that academic institutions should be more deliberate in their efforts to promote good mentoring relationships for students and junior faculty, particularly for those who have historically been excluded. The advantages of male sponsor/protégé relationships have long been supported and maintained, and institutions have a responsibility to compensate. While it may appear that sponsor/protégé relationships occur naturally between people of similar interests outside of the realm of institutional action, the significant tendency for members of certain groups to be excluded, and thereby disadvantaged, indicates that they do not occur randomly or haphazardly. Thus institutions truly committed to promoting equity for women and other minorities must take action to ensure their inclusion in these relationships.

They can do so through a two-pronged approach. First, top administrators within the institution must take an active role in legitimizing and rewarding faculty members' efforts to provide sponsorship to junior members of the community. This may be done through public communications such as talks, letters, and goal and policy statements, through setting a positive example as a sponsor themselves, and through actually having faculty sponsorship count as a factor in tenure, promotion, and salary decisions. This support is also shown in the types of organizations and networks which are recognized and utilized by top administrators. If various women's formal and informal associations are frequently consulted in the normal course of institutional decision-making, for example, then they are likely to be perceived as having merit and legitimacy, and thus are likely to attract potential sponsors and protégés to a setting where those relationships may flourish. In addition, closer contact by top administrators and senior faculty with these networks provides greater access for women to institutional influence and information, including the unwritten, yet essential, rules of behavior and practice.

Second, institutions must take an active role in helping students and junior faculty understand the value of having a sponsor, and in assisting them in the process of identifying and "cultivating" one. This may be accomplished through informal activities, discussions, and networks which may serve to bring together people of similar interests. Some have suggested actually assigning mentors to beginning students, although others argue that the relationship flourishes when initiated by either or both parties. Increasing internship opportunities may expand formal helping relationships between experts and beginners in a field. Peer advising programs and written guides, or "paper mentors," can provide essential survival manuals on the unwritten policies and practices at the institution. In addition, students should be encouraged to seek out "multiple mentors," so that they can benefit from what a number of people have to offer, rather than put all their reliance on one person (Hall and Sandler 1983).

Several institutions, including the Massachusetts Institute of Technology and City University of New York, have already begun to encourage and support the formation of sponsor/protégé relationships among students who might previously be excluded from them. At other institutions, many women and women's groups have recognized the importance of these ties, and have actively and deliberately sought to develop and maintain them, although this takes time, energy, and conflict if women are torn between male and female organizations. In any case, it seems clear that rather than attempt to negate a relationship which has provided advantages to one group, institutions and individuals are better served by trying to extend those advantages to all. Because institutions have played an active role in supporting and maintaining the benefits derived by white males from the current sponsorship system, they should play an equal or greater role in opening that system to others.

Sponsors and Tokens

But they should always be aware that sponsorship is not always formed in a way that serves the best interests of women. Judith Long Laws described the sponsor/token relationship for faculty, in which the male sponsor integrates the female into a dominant group. (Laws has a specific definition of the token role that is somewhat different from Kanter's.) The sponsor helps the token manage her double-deviant status—being female, and being a female academic—although both the token and the sponsor agree that the token represents an exceptional member of her group. The paradoxical position requires that the token be less likely to be aware of her deviant status than the members of the dominant group. She sees herself as "one of the boys" although they never forget that she's a woman, for whom sex-related cues are more salient than task-related cues (Laws 1975).

This dynamic endures particularly when dominant groups are under pressure to include minority group members. The token's presence serves many functions for the dominant group. Her presence supports their belief in their profession as a meritocracy. Her inclusion demonstrates that if only women were excellent enough, they could achieve group membership. The dominant group members can then feel secure in their lack of prejudice against women. According to Laws, the token is often put in a position of providing boundary maintenance for the group, of screening out other women so that the dominant group members can feel further satisfaction that their processes are unbiased because, after all, a woman herself made the negative decisions. This may be done by making her a part of department hiring decisions, for example, or a member of the admissions committee. Her very presence relieves the dominant group members, at least in their own minds, of responsibility for seriously considering female candidates, particularly potentially disruptive ones, at all. Furthermore, the sponsor initiates the token in such a way so that she never disrupts the functioning of the group or challenges its standards or values, but rather learns to find an appropriate niche for herself, generally along sex role-related lines in a position of "permanent marginality" (Laws 1975). Thus, not only does the role of token inhibit the participation of other women and perpetuate a biased system, but it inhibits the token's own professional development as well.

In her book, *Women in Science*, Vivian Gornick refers to this phenomenon in her description of the attitude and demeanor of the older women scientists whom she interviewed. These women spent the bulk of their professional lives working within heavily male-dominated environments. A woman scientist was not just an anomaly, but almost a contradiction in terms:

> In the past, differences in style, personality, character were not permitted women scientists, and so none were exhibited. A woman scientist of only thirty years ago was a lady eccentric. . . . Adopting the style of the gentlemen scientists among whom they worked, these women acceded in a socially repressive atmosphere to an even deeper repression of the self.
>
> An overwhelming majority of the women scientists I spoke with who were between the ages of sixty-five and

eighty-five conformed to the stereotype. Regardless of background or actual experience, there was about them a uniform remoteness of manner and expression. The pose was haughty and aristocratic, the speech guarded, the personality masked, defensive, unknowing. Each of them, in effect, said to me: "Problem? My dear, I *had* no problem. I knew what I wanted to do, and I simply did it." Caricatures of intellectual reserve and neutered sexuality, they would not discuss why they had never married, why they had worked as associates for fifty years, why they had been treated like den mothers and mascots by their colleagues.

In one study, there was a significant correlation for all the faculty women surveyed between having a sponsor in graduate school or work, and faculty rank. Those women the authors designated as tokens (defined as scoring above the median on an Academic System Belief Scale, below the median on questions on sex discrimination, and reporting no membership in feminist organizations) were the same age as the others, but were more likely to have tenure, and tended to hold higher rank (Young et al. 1980). If having a sponsor leads to greater academic rewards for women, those who can be classified as tokens reap rewards to an even greater degree. The somewhat greater rewards of token women suggest either that the system tends to better reward those whose behavior and attitudes are least disruptive or challenging, or that those who have been most successful are more likely to believe in the system and less likely to identify discrimination.

Sexual Harassment

Not only does the sponsor/protégé relationship seem to occur less frequently for women than for men, but in some cases, it may take a different form as well. In acting as protégés, women may in some cases be participating in an interaction meant to inhibit rather than encourage their development and that of other women.

Nowhere is the potential damage caused by harmful informal interactions between senior men and junior women more apparent than in cases of sexual harassment. Generally, sexual harassment is understood to mean unwanted sexual attention or advances which inhibit or interfere with the victim's work or study. Each institution which has addressed the issue of sexual harassment develops its own policy and definition, and even within those perameters, debate and disagreement promote varied interpretations and judgments of individual acts. According to one analyst, for a definition to be useful in both educating the community and potential and current harassers, and in providing legal ammunition to victims, it should "recognize a wide range of behavior and experiences as sexual harassment," and "acknowledge a potentially broad impact and effect on victims" (Crocker 1983). The National Advisory Council on Women's Educational Programs developed the following working definition of sexual harassment for students:

> Academic sexual harassment is the use of authority to emphasize the sexuality or sexual identity of a student in a manner which prevents or impairs that student's full enjoyment of educational benefits, climate, or opportunity. [Till 1980]

From this definition, they classified five types of activities as sexual harassment:

> 1) Generalized sexist remarks or behavior;
> 2) Inappropriate and offensive but essentially sanction-free sexual advances;
> 3) Solicitation of sexual activity or other sex-linked behavior by promise of rewards;
> 4) Coercion of sexual activity by threat of punishment;
> 5) Sexual assaults. [Till 1980]

The Equal Opportunity Commission published the following definition of sexual harassment, which would apply to employees of colleges and universities:

> Unwelcome sexual advances, requests for sexual favors and other verbal and physical conduct of a sexual nature . . . when:
>
> 1. Submission to such conduct is made either explicitly or implicitly a term or condition of an individual's employment;
> 2. submission to or rejection of such conduct by an individual is used as the basis for employment decision affecting such individual, or

3. such conduct has the purpose of unreasonably in-
terfering with an individual's work performance or
creating an intimidating, hostile or offensive work
environment.

The phenomenon of sexual harassment presents many problems
for women in academia, as they are far more likely than men to be
the victims of it, to hear about it from students, and to be vulnerable
in reporting it. Because, as students or junior faculty members and
as women within male-dominated institutions, they are less likely
to be in positions of power, women maneuver their way through
land mines of subtle and blatant harassment, attempting to mini-
mize the damage to themselves and their careers. For every woman
willing to come forward with a complaint, scores have to endure
discomfort. Many abandon their work due to the intrusion of a
sexual agenda by a person with some sort of power over the progress
or success of their careers. While faculty/student relationships were
once considered an expected, if not romantic, facet of campus life,
the negative impact of these liaisons, even those begun with the
full consent of both parties, is beginning to be understood. A recent
survey of Harvard students and faculty reveals the extent to which
these relationships occur. Thirty-two percent of the tenured female
professors, 49 percent of those without tenure, 41 percent of the
female graduate students, and 34 percent of the undergraduate
women reported having been sexually harassed by a person in
authority at least once during their time at Harvard. (McCain1983).
Fifteen percent of the graduate students and twelve percent of the
undergraduates reporting harassment consequently changed their
academic plans because of it. Most did not report the incidents. Half
feared reprisals if they did so. A similar study of 1446 women and
men at the University of Pennsylvania showed that 26.4 percent of
the female undergraduates, 30 percent of the female graduate or
professional students, 41.6 percent of the female faculty, and 33.1
percent of the female staff reported experiencing sexual harassment
over the previous five years from persons in authority. Only a tiny
percentage of women reporting harassment on the survey (less than
6 percent of graduate students, less than 3 percent of faculty women,
and no undergraduate students or staff women) had made formal
complaints, perhaps illustrating their lack of faith in the institution
to respond in a fair and helpful way. There is no reason to expect
that similar percentages would not exist on other campuses. The

ramifications of the injection of sex into the academic sphere is even more damaging than the frequency of actual incidents seems to indicate. Even if a woman does not abandon her academic plans, the harassment reminds her that she is seen primarily as a sexual rather than an intellectual being, and that, in fact, she is at the mercy of a male-dominated institution.

Despite the high level of frequency of incidents of sexual harassment, many resist institutionalized efforts to combat it. Some neglect to see the element of power in these interactions, and feel that they are personal matters outside of the rightful purview of institutional policy. Others fear that apprehension about the appearance or accusation of harassment may even further inhibit the establishment of mentoring relationships between senior men and junior women faculty and students. Some others fear that strong institutionalized attempts to provide vehicles for complaints would lead to an onslaught of unjustified accusations. Others are troubled by the fine points of the definition of harassment, i.e. the implications of mutual consent, the interpretation of various behaviors, or the prosecutability of generalized sexist remarks. These questions plague campuses where attempts have been made to merely articulate a unified stand on this issue, let alone to develop a clear, coherent, and workable policy and grievance procedure. Even among those committed to combating harassment, there has been disagreement as to the proper and best way to do so. There is general agreement within these ranks, however, that nothing short of strong community and institutional action will begin to make a dent in this problem. Without it, statements decrying its harmfulness lack meaning, and women will continue to be left with the burden of coping individually and suffering personal and professional disadvantage by these actions.

Institutions need to keep in mind three primary goals, formulated by a committee at Hunter College of the City University of New York: "a) the hearing and possible resolution of sexual harassment complaints brought by students, faculty, and staff, b) education of the community concerning what sexual harassment is, and c) informing the college community that such behavior will not be tolerated" (Polakoff 1984). The American Association of University Professors offers suggested guidelines for dealing with sexual harassment which emphasize confidentiality, informal resolution of complaints, and reliance on institutional grievance procedures currently in place (A.A.U.P. 1983). Separate from the obvious benefits of settling complaints quickly and quietly, for the complainant and the harasser, institutions need to be mindful of the powerful message which is conveyed throughout the community by the strength of their actions. The appearance and reality of fair decision-making processes, visible support for victims, a broad and workable definition, and meaningful penalties for harassers have a broader impact than merely the resolution of individual cases, as they signal a genuine institutional commitment to recognizing its responsibility for combatting this problem and addressing it in strong and direct ways.

Indeed, institutions need to be mindful of their role and their responsibility for addressing all of the issues raised by the interactions between senior faculty and junior faculty and students as they relate to the status of women. While it may be easy to reject the need or appropriateness of institutional intervention because of the personal or subjective nature of these relationships (and in fact this has often been used as a rationale for lack of institutional involvement), the temptation should be resisted—if only because of the formal and informal ways in which institutions have systematically supported men in the positive aspects of these interactions, and have protected them in the harmful ones.

Top administrators must recognize how the system of informal relationships favors men, and develop ways to equalize these benefits. They must accept responsibility for airing the dirty linen of sexual harassment, and create processes to protect victims, meaningfully penalize harassers, and send out a clear message that such behavior is unacceptable within the community. On the positive side, they must create ways to support the sponsorship of women, by both encouraging and rewarding senior faculty who do so, and by providing vehicles through which junior women can connect with potential mentors. Institutions must take deliberate action to ensure equity for women scholars, rather than operating in a manner which results in the de facto exclusion of women from the benefits of these relationships. They cannot claim that they have no role to play, for not acting represents a choice which endorses the current balance in favor of men.

Top administrators must make it their business to recognize and support the positive impact of the sponsorship of women in the provision of intellectual stimulation, successful example, career assistance, political savvy, and emotional support. Given the particular difficulties still present for women aspiring to academic careers, it is especially important that adequate numbers of women within each department serve in this role, as role models and guides to help women navigate their way through the predominantly male academic world. This is not to absolve men of their responsibility to sponsor women. Men continue to be better connected than women to the political and intellectual networks within fields and institutions. They offer essential benefits to beginning scholars. In addition, it should not be assumed that women all will have similar academic interests. Rather, institutions must devise ways to extend the same range of options currently available to male scholars to female scholars.

There is a limited amount of research suggesting that women may perceive and implement the role of sponsor differently than men. It seems that they may have a more personal relationship with their students, but a less productive, work-oriented one. This was supported by the anecdotes of the women interviewed for this study, who reported that students were more likely to come to them than their male colleagues for personal problems or moral support. If indeed this is true, it seems that both men and women could benefit from some borrowing from each other's style. A fundamental component in the issue of sponsorship is the tendency for the faculty woman to continue to be perceived as a role anomaly. This situation will be ameliorated somewhat by an increase in the numbers of faculty women, in addition to the numbers of women in other historically male-dominated professions, thus making women less of a rarity in these fields. However, numbers alone, while helpful, will not change attitudes, erase stereotypes, and reverse practices which have prevailed for more than three centuries in American higher education, particularly if the power continues to rest in the hands of men. It will take genuine commitment and direct action from those with the power to bestow and withhold rewards within the institution to ensure women's inclusion as full members in the academic community and as full recipients of its multitude of benefits and rewards.

6
Marital Status and Academic Women

It's been just awful. I wish I was a sixty year old man with a wife who types. It's a terrible situation.

—*interview with a faculty woman*

It was hard when the children were growing up, because I was always ambitious and determined. Yes, I really wanted children, but I wouldn't hand over my life to them. I just couldn't. So I felt a lot of conflict in the early years.

—*interview with a faculty woman*

Although the contemporary feminist movement has challenged the division of labor within the home and the workplace, women are still expected to take primary responsibility for the well-being of the home and family. Whether women and men accept, reject, or modify this expectation, it still has an impact on their careers and their lives.

In some ways, the relatively flexible schedule of academic life seems well-suited to the needs of women with kin-related responsibilities, such as husbands and children. Yet this impression is deceptive. The demands for devotion to research and scholarship can leave less non-job-related time than a more rigid nine-to-five schedule. In many other ways as well, the life choices of academic women have effects on their careers that set them apart from academic men and from other professional women. This chapter will examine how academic women perceive, and are affected by, the issues of marital and family status.

In 1964, although there had recently been an increase in the percentage of married academic women, Bernard found academic women less likely to be married than academic men, or other professional women. A study at one institution showed that 93 percent of the men but only 46 percent of the women were married; at another, the figures were 94.7 and 56.8 (Eckert and Stecklein 1961; Bryan and Boring 1947). Academic women were also less likely to be married than women with comparable training in other professions. Among female doctorates in biology, for example, 56 percent of those in nonacademic positions were married, compared to only 29 percent in academic positions (Bernard 1964).

In addition, the marriages of academic women were less stable than those of academic men, with higher divorce rates for academic women than for academic men or for the general population (Bryan and Boring 1947; Jacobson 1959). Various studies also showed that academic women reported less satisfaction with their marriages than academic men, with 91.7 percent of the men, compared with 79.4 percent of the women, being satisfied or enthusiastic about their marriages (Bryan and Boring).

Needless to say, the experiences of married academic women were not the same as those of married academic men. In 1964, as today, women bore sole or primary responsibility for the home and family. It was assumed that women would perform their wife and mother roles at least adequately before performing others, just as it was assumed that men would give most of their attention to performing their professional roles. In addition to these assumptions, wives were expected to provide whatever assistance and support was necessary to further their husbands' careers. Married academic women, many of whom felt that their careers were a luxury or a privilege, could not expect and perhaps did not demand similar types of support. Indeed, women and men did not view their marriages in the same way with respect to their careers. A 1947 study of psychologists found that 28 percent of the full-time women saw their marriage as a professional asset, compared to 72 percent of the married men, while 34 percent of the women, and only 5 percent of the men, saw their marriage as a hindrance. Twenty-five percent of the women saw their children as professional assets, while 60 percent saw them as professional liabilities (Bryan and Boring).

The modern feminist movement has devoted a great deal of attention to the interaction between women's careers and their marital and family status, and to the ways in which institutions and individuals can support the choices made in this realm. One would expect, then, that the situation had changed for academic women nearly twenty years later. Yet the research continues to show that academic women, both faculty and graduate students, are less likely to be married and have children than are academic men. One study of male and female graduate students showed that only 29 percent of the married females were full-time students, compared to 50.9 percent of the married men (Feldman 1974). Once having received the doctorate, women are still less likely to be married, although among the more recent graduates, the trend seems to be moving in the direction of marriage for women. For example, 47.9 percent of female 1968 Ph.D. recipients had married only once, compared to 35 percent of 1950 and 1960 graduates. This is in contrast, however, to 81.2 percent of the male 1968 graduates, and 78.5 percent of those graduating in 1950 and 1960. Similarly, 30 percent of the female 1968 graduates never married, compared to 7.6 percent of the males (Centra 1975).

These differences between academic women and men exist, to a greater or lesser extent, in nearly every academic discipline. In an analysis of science and engineering fields, men had a higher marriage rate than women in every field but physics and astronomy, with an overall rate of 67.2 percent for men and 51.4 percent for women (N.R.C. 1979). The same holds true for different types of institutions. At Quality I institutions, for example, 40 percent of the women, while only 8 percent of the men, were single (Freeman 1977). Among top level academic administrators in one study, ten times as many women as men were never married, twice as many women as men were divorced, four times as many women as men were separated or widowed, and five times as many women as men had no children (Andruskiw and Howe 1980). As in Bernard's time, those marriages that do exist for academic women seem to be less stable than those of academic men.

Effect of Marriage and Children on Employment Status

Not surprisingly, the weight of the research seems to indicate that marriage is beneficial to the careers of academic men, but not to those of academic women.

On the whole, women with doctorates tend to be unemployed in greater numbers than men with doctorates. However, while more women than men may prefer unemployed status (5.6 percent versus 2.4 percent), far more women are unemployed than would prefer it (11.1 percent for women, 3.8 percent for men) (Centra 1974). This is even more true for married women, particularly those with children.

In one study, when asked for reasons for current unemployment, 40 percent of the women and none of the men gave reasons related to marital status ("spouse did not want me to work," "anti-nepotism policies," and "no suitable job for spouse") or to domestic responsibilities ("pregnant," "no day care"). Fifty-seven percent of the women gave responses such as these to explain periods of past unemployment, while none of the men did (Centra). In another study, even among those who were employed, married women in the biomedical and behavioral sciences were more likely than those of any other group to hold jobs which were unrelated to their academic training (N.R.C. 1977).

For those who work in academic careers, marriage seems to be related to professional success for men more so than women. For example, at Quality I institutions, of those males still married to their first wives, 38 percent were full professors, 22 percent associate professors, and 28 percent assistant professors. For women still married to their first husbands, 6 percent were full professors, 12 percent associate professors, 36 percent assistant professors, and 46 percent were instructors or lecturers. Of men who never married, 15 percent were full professors, 18 percent associate professors, and 41 percent assistant professors, while of women who never married, 17 percent were full professors, 23 percent were associate professors, 30 percent were assistant professors, and 30 percent were instructors or lecturers (Freeman). While these statistics may be confounded by the age of men and women at the different ranks, it seems that not only having a job, but progressing within that job, is related to having a spouse in a way that is positive for men and negative for women. Not surprisingly, academic men tend to have more children than academic women as well (Centra).

All of these figures do not even begin to account for the women who do not begin, or interrupt, or abandon their academic careers at the graduate level, due to marital and domestic pressures. One study, done in 1971, of 1,961 freshmen who had gone on to graduate school showed that 24 percent of the women, as opposed to 15 percent of the men, listed family obligations as obstacles to completing their studies, and 44 percent of the women, compared with

17 percent of the men, listed home/child care responsibilities as reasons for interrupting study (El-Khawas and Bisconti, 1974). Another study of Woodrow Wilson Fellows from 1958 to 1962 showed a dramatic increase in the dropout rate for women with children, with no comparable gap for men (Solmon 1973).

The research shows clearly that marriage and family, while having a positive effect on the careers of men, has a negative effect on the progress of women's careers. Married women, particularly with children, are more likely to have dropped out of graduate school, have interrupted or abandoned their careers, be unemployed or employed in a job unrelated to their training, or to hold lower academic rank.

Effect of Marriage and Children on Attitudes and Performance

To a large extent, the reward system of academia is based on the quality and quantity of research efforts. One of the explanations given for the generally lower status for women is their lower rate of research productivity as compared to men. One might guess that the larger the woman's nonprofessional time commitments and responsibilities, the less likely she would be to be able to devote a great amount of effort to her scholarship efforts. Therefore, women with smaller families, or no families, would seem to be at an advantage. However, the findings on the effect of marriage and children on women's research productivity are mixed.

Despite one study which showed a somewhat stronger interest in teaching for married women (Feldman), several studies found no difference between married and single women in publication rates. An analysis of the results of an American Council on Education survey of college and university faculty found that after controlling all factors, women published 25 percent fewer articles than did men, but that neither marital status nor numbers of children had an effect on either productivity or on the probability of being listed as outstanding (Hamovitch and Morgenstern 1977). This general conclusion was also supported by Cole, who examined faculty in the sciences (Cole 1979), and by Freeman at Quality I institutions.

On the other hand, Astin and Bayer (1979) found that contrary to the popular conception, married women were more productive than single women. They found the careers of married women to be more comparable to those of married men than were single women's with respect to their educational preparation, field of study, and publications, although this finding may be confounded by the additional age and seniority of married women. This was reinforced by greater salary differentials between predicted and actual salaries for single women than for married women.

While virtually all authors refer to the difficulties women face trying to carry out scholarly and domestic activities, the data do not show that a difference exists in actual productivity for married women, or women with children compared to single women. There are several possible explanations for this seeming lack of consistency.

One is that those women who are most likely to allow their domestic responsibilities to interfere with their academic work have been sifted out before they reach the faculty ranks— either by dropping out voluntarily or by receiving less active support and encouragement in their career moves. Thus, only those married women who are willing to put their primary effort into their careers are able to survive in faculty positions. This would obscure the documented impact of family and children, and would make the records of these women similar to those of single women.

A second explanation, not in opposition to the first one, is that married women with families are able to keep their productivity up to the same level as single women, but at enormous costs to themselves. One could speculate that these women devote huge amounts of time and effort to their domestic *and* their professional lives, leaving little or no time for activities not immediately related to either world. A study on psychologist couples lends some support to this idea, as the wives related that time was a major dissatisfaction for them, particularly with regard to those activities, such as interactions with colleagues, pursuing long-range job goals, and avocations, not related to day-to-day pressing demands (Bryson et al. 1978). Perhaps married faculty women are succeeding, but at a higher sacrifice than other groups endure. One faculty women writes:

> Even the most solidly competent men—those who do not aspire to originality or profoundity—have that sweet freedom, the freedom of time and movement, that schedule-juggling women do not have. We all need time for sheer musing, for reading novels, playing music, wandering about the river. And this is precisely what efficient scholarly women do not have . . . We cannot respect our ec-

centricities, cannot honor them where they may lead us.
[Rorty 1977]

A third explanation is that many of these married faculty women simply do not accept the traditional female role of full responsibility for domestic activities, or that those who accept responsibility are aided by husbands, children, relatives, and hired help. These various possible domestic arrangements will be discussed in more depth later in this chapter.

Part of the explanation for the lower productivity of women is that they are excluded from networks of informal communication. In one study of graduate students, 21 percent more married women than married men and 18 percent more married women than single women responded affirmatively to the statement, "Almost none of the people I see socially are fellow students in my department" (Feldman).

However, there is also evidence that while married women are less a part of informal networks of communication than are single women, those networks in which they are involved may tend to be less homogeneous and to include more men. Kaufman found that while single women had larger networks of colleague-friends, they were less likely to have men in their networks, as they suffered from a greater stigma of deviancy and did not carry the "protective status" of being married (Kaufman 1978). Married academic women may be more acceptable to faculty men because at least the women are in one familiar role, and because the sexual issue is resolved, at least publicly. However, married women may also be taken less seriously, as it may be assumed that their roles as wives and mothers are primary for them, and that they consequently have less career dedication. One faculty member spoke of the complex consequences of being single with respect to informal relationships with colleagues.

> I guess in a way it made them take me more seriously, because they have this stupid fantasy that married women are always dusting the silverware, or something. And it probably meant that they saw me as very sexless, which was good. But then, on the other hand, it didn't work that way because some of them tend to see married women as more sexless, because they're sexually taken care of and I was kind of disruptive, you know, at lunch or some-

> thing. . . . It is very hard to have lunch with a colleague in this department face to face. Still, they're very shy and nervous. They don't know how to treat you. I think if I were married they would see me as not sexually on the prowl. I mean, they have these fantasies and I can't read their fantasies. Lately, all the new women in the department are married and with children, and they get a certain kind of approval that I never got. But I think it might be approval laced with condescension. I mean, what you're really asking me to do is enter the minds of these extremely inhibited and conventional and sexist people, who are yet very decent. When I start trying to read their projections onto me or any of us, I just give up in despair.

Marital status has an influence on informal interactions in a number of different ways. Married women may be less likely than single women to socialize with colleagues, due to conflicting time demands. Yet they may be more free in those friendships which they do form, particularly with men, as their marital status makes them less threatening to men than single women are. What is clear is that both married and single women may be at a disadvantage in informal networks, albeit in somewhat different ways.

Also related to productivity is the extent to which one sees oneself as a scholar. A study of scholarly-eminence ambition in graduate students showed that being married was related to higher ambition for both sexes, except for women with young children, who subscribed to traditional female roles (Acker 1977). Being married with young children may be a constraint, perhaps temporarily, to women in their ability to be or to see themselves as professional academics, with their attitudes regarding appropriate female roles as the determining factor. While the stereotype may be that married academic women really do not take themselves or their careers seriously, the reality may be more complicated. Married women may take their careers as seriously as men do, provided their own attitudes deem career dedication as appropriate for women and available supports allow them to do so. Because they are not nearly as likely to have spouses to take care of domestic details, they do not have the luxury that married men might of subordinating all aspects of their lives to their work.

Another way in which seriousness about career has been judged by others, often to the detriment of women, is by the extent of career mobility. At least until recently, there was a tradition of men, from all types of careers, uprooting their families for professional advancement. This tradition resulted in the expectation that one *must* move to demonstrate seriousness and ambition.

There is some evidence to support the notion that a married women's location is still dominated to a certain extent by her husband's needs. One study of 107 academic couples showed that while a proportion of the job location decisions were equalitarian or female-led, husbands still were more likely than wives to determine where the couple would live. Women were also more likely to agree with the statement, "If I weren't married, I would have been able to obtain a better position" (Wallston et al. 1978). In another study, women in all fields were significantly more likely to see their husbands as major deterrents to considering a job in another community, while men were significantly more likely not to see their wives as deterrents at all (Centra 1974).

While there is some evidence to support the notion of lesser mobility for married women, the reasons for this are by no means situated in the individual women. Some couples may indeed be motivated by the traditional value that the husband's career should be the primary one within the family, and that the family should be located accordingly, leaving it to the wife, if she wants to work at all, to find the most acceptable position within commuting range of her husband's job.

On the other hand, these decisions may be economically motivated. If men are likely, for a number of reasons, to receive better job offers or more money for the same jobs, then a couple may have to choose between an excellent offer for the husband in one location and a mediocre one for the wife in another. It seems unlikely that the wife's position would win out in that case, even if the couple attempted to make an equalitarian decision. So perhaps, at least to some extent, the lesser mobility of women is linked to a system which offers families higher incentives to pursue the husband's opportunities than the wife's, rather than on a conscious decision by the wife to subordinate her career to her husband's. This presents an alternative to the argument that women are unable to make job commitments because they are afraid or unwilling to do so.

Two important factors in the relationship between marriage and career for academic women are the degree to which the wife and husband accept traditional sex roles and the extent to which formal and informal policies and practices support the choices individuals have made. If the woman subscribes to nontraditional attitudes, for example, she is more likely to make arrangements to share the domestic responsibilities, or to dedicate herself to her research, or to be willing to uproot her family to change to a better job for herself. Married women continue to be, overall, somewhat at a disadvantage, unless they are willing to see their relationship to career and family in a nontraditional way and can get their families to do the same. Unlike married men, these women must make double adaptations and sacrifices to accommodate both roles and to keep others from being uncomfortable. The following section will discuss those adaptations.

Individual Adaptations

The personal accounts of academic women, whether in interviews for this study or in written accounts elsewhere, show the various ways women have responded and adapted to issues raised by marital status and children.

Some women, for a number of reasons, do not choose to get married. The literature shows that this may be more likely to be true for academic women than for women in general. One of the single women in this study described her decision to remain so as the result of her inability to find a relationship in which she would truly be seen as an equal partner.

> I'm single. I have explored relations in the past. . . . A lot of the marriage proposals I turned down have basically been—"You say all the right things about equality, but you don't act all the right ways, and your actions speak infinitely louder than your words."

For women who have attained high levels of achievement within professional spheres, it may be even more difficult to play a subordinate role in their relationships. Many women do, however, put the careers of their husbands before their own, or at least structure their careers in such a way as to fit neatly with those of their husbands.

The most obvious case, of course, are women who abandon their careers altogether. Some, in addition to providing emotional and domestic support to their husbands, are able, due to their own training, to provide intellectual and scholarly support as well. In this arrangement, in addition to providing direct benefits to the husband, a woman's training and intelligence are not totally lost to the system. Also, the wife is able to feel that she is making a contribution, albeit at a lower level than if she were pursuing her own career. However, this relationship is set up in such a way that the system benefits from her contributions at a relatively low cost, while she remains virtually invisible and receives very few concrete rewards.

Another way in which academic women subordinate their own professional careers to their husbands' is by teaching or doing research part-time at the institutions at which their husbands are affiliated. Often denied full-time positions because of anti-nepotism policies or lack of openings, these women are able to remain somewhat professionally active. The benefits to the institution are enormous, as it has a more or less captive pool of talent from which to draw at very little cost in money, status, or professional benefits.

Of the women interviewed for this study, none was currently in the above-described situation, as they were all, by sampling definition, full-time faculty members. Additionally, holding a faculty post at a major Quality I institution can hardly be considered making a major career sacrifice. Nonetheless, even within this group, many made their choice of career or of location dependent upon their husbands'.

> I got married, and then I came to P_____. That's why I came to P_____, because my husband was doing graduate work here.

> We have to find a place where we can both be—P_____ is one place . . . It is a problem because I've already had chances to go to other states and I've said no.

Another faculty member described rushing through her doctoral program, and then making a commitment to remain at P_____, to accommodate her career to her husband's. She continued:

> It also pushed me strongly to try to get tenure here as opposed to exploring other options. And to do what it took to get tenure as opposed to any place else, as I was feeling landlocked. This is clearly, if I live in L_____, the best job opportunity I have in L_____. So I think in those terms.

In the following account, a faculty member, who had had nine different interruptions in her training and her work to either follow her husband in his career or to have children, stated:

> Well, I'm a rather classic case of a woman who began with a graduate program and a profession and ended up following her husband from one place to another, and was forced to give up one project or one educational activity after another. . . . I was cross being at B_____ because I had started out at better schools. And I didn't really have a choice—I had two kids and I couldn't really make the drive to C_____.

As this woman described, having children further complicates the tug women feel, but men do not feel, between family and career. First of all, they must perform within the traditional male model of having someone at home to tend to most of the domestic and childraising responsibilities.

> I think there's a whole set of expectations that come from males assuming there's someone else at home taking basic responsibility for the kids and that that affects not just when they schedule meetings, but expectations about where your total energies are put and how much time you're going to have to devote to things. I don't think I've run into real overt discrimination except when I was job hunting . . . Since then, I really think the issues revolve around the dual role thing.

One women delayed having her first child until after she had tenure, because she realized that she would be unable to do all the necessary research if she had a child competing for her time. It is interesting to note that while she enjoys her son, she would have been willing to forego parenthood if her career was not at a point with which she was satisfied.

> It meant I couldn't have children until I had tenure here, and I postponed that decision until then. I was quite willing not to have children if I didn't get tenure. . . . It's cut back my research effort about 90 percent. I would be a nervous wreck if I didn't have tenure.

On the other hand, all of the other interviewed women with children had their children first, and then adapted their careers. One, who described her situation as "awful," outlined her plans to combine her work and her year-old daughter during the upcoming year.

> This is how I'm resolving my conflict. My child is taking too much of my time and I need to finish my book before I come up for tenure. I'm taking childcare leave to finish my book, to get some childcare from family members who can take care of the baby while I work, because I don't want to put her in an institution full time. My husband is real supportive of this. What the future holds— I must finish my book and I will. Probably tenure or not, I'll have another child because I don't think money should interfere with important issues in my life.

Two of the other women simply interrupted their careers altogether when their children were young, and then structured their careers around their children. Another woman found her department to be willing to be flexible with her hours, so that she could continue working. It should be noted that this was an adaptation arranged to respond to her individual case, rather than a structural adaptation demonstrating institutional support for faculty members with children. Another simply combined the two roles in their entirety, trying to devote her total attention to each in turn, while keeping them separate.

All of the married women but one described their marriages as being at least somewhat nontraditional. This manifested itself in a number of different ways. Some lived four to five hours away from their husbands during the week. Others described wholly equalitarian job searches, in which the couple lived equidistant between their two jobs, or in which the husband followed her to an educational program and job. Several had husbands with flexible job schedules, which allowed shared child care and domestic responsibilities. Many claimed to have no clear roles around the house.

Yet it seemed that the women still assumed the major responsibility for the household and family. Even though their husbands were helpful and supportive, the women seemed to be the ones who saw those responsibilities and functions as their own. Clearly, their careers were more noticeably affected by them, and they made more career sacrifices for family than did their husbands. Two of the women, who claimed to have husbands who were active in child and household-related activities, described their situations in this way:

> I get real tired, and I have to make a lot of arrangements so people can eat and have clean clothes and it gets real tiring. If I was single, it would be very different. But I'm happy with what I have and wouldn't want to give it up.

> I realize, I'm coming to the sense now, that I might not have the career I planned for myself—that ability has nothing to do with it and that I'm going to lose ground because I'm a woman. My husband will lose some because he has to split some of the responsibilities. But ultimately, I'm going to lose more because I keep a lot of the details of life together that he doesn't think of.

Regardless of the demands of their own careers, the willingness of husbands to share domestic responsibilities, and the changes in attitudes about the role of women, these academic women were operating on the assumption and reality that basic responsibility for the maintenance and well-being of the family fell to them. In almost every case where a conflict arose, their careers were somehow accommodated to their families, rather than the other way around. They did not describe many situations in which this had been the case for their husbands. While many described their husbands as supportive, this generally meant that they were accepting, and even encouraging, of their wives' desire to assume both roles. Their help around the house was simply that—help for their wives in performing their wives' role. While this may have reflected the way these women preferred to structure their lives, academia continues to be structured as if all faculty members had someone at home performing the functions of a traditional wife.

However, it should be noted that virtually all of the married women were involved in somewhat nontraditional marriages. Without the degree of flexibility that was present, and the attitudes there to support it, it seems unlikely that these women would have achieved the high level of professional success that they did. One must wonder about the personal costs these women paid, and about the many other talented women who were left by the wayside because they were expected to perform functions that their male competitors did not have to concern themselves with.

The academic women in this study represent success stories in many ways. They have been able to make arrangements that have been workable for themselves and their families, and they have achieved a high level of professional success, by any standards. Yet their success has been based on their own individual abilities to cope, adapt, and arrange their lives, and on at least some measure of cooperation from those around them, including husbands, department heads, advisors, and children. The responsibility of creating workable systems rested solely on them, as did the ultimate responsibility for domestic functions. Individual solutions, rather than institutional ones, have been the key to these women's success.

Institutional Supports and Barriers

The research thus far indicates that the academic system is based on assumptions, attitudes, and policies which are more likely to benefit men than women. Men are systematically advantaged by having institutionalized supports both at home and at work that are closely adapted to their needs and experience. Arlie Russell Hochschild has described them as "the very clockwork of a career system that seems to eliminate women not so much through malevolent disobedience to good rules, but through making up rules to suit half of the population" (Hochschild 1975).

This is nowhere more evident than with regard to the effect of marriage and children on career. The academic workplace, along with most others, is contructed on the assumption that there is someone else at home to attend to one's domestic and family needs. Married men may have the benefit of a two-person career, when one considers the direct or indirect assistance of a wife, while married women are more likely to be part of a two-career couple. While there may be no conscious attempt to discriminate, if the effect is such that one group has an advantage over the other, the intent, if indeed it is benign, is irrelevant. Sexism is present when institutionalized power is combined with prejudice against women. Within academia, the effects of sexism have been particularly strong against married women, as the system has been even less responsive to their needs.

There are a number of ways in which this is true. Receiving fellowships, assistantships, grants, and benefits can be even more difficult for married women than for single, based on the questionable assumptions that married women have husbands to support them and do not need the money and that married women will direct their energy and commitment towards their families rather than their work, and therefore giving them a share of limited financial resources is wasteful, as they will contribute less to their disciplines and will perhaps drop out altogether. Holding similar attitudes and practices for married men would be considered absurd, not to mention unfair.

Another form of discrimination against married women occurs when the woman's husband is also affiliated with the institution. For years, many institutions had anti-nepotism policies, which generally prohibited married faculty couples from working either in the same department or at the same institution. At face value, the policies existed to prevent unwanted alliances and conflicts, as well as to prevent unfair preference to family members in hiring decisions. However, because the men tended to be in more senior positions, or because they were simply more highly valued by their departments, the policies served to disadvantage academic women, particularly those whose husbands were employed at isolated institutions, with few opportunities in the surrounding area for their employment. What may have seemed at first glance to be a sound and fair policy, at closer examination proved to be a mechanism through which sexist discrimination occurred.

When it was in the best interest of the institution, however, the arguments against having husbands and wives working together seemed less compelling to those in decision-making positions. For example, wives were often hired in part-time or non-tenure-track positions. When it came to providing equal status and rewards for those wives, however, the arguments reemerged.

Over the past several years, the deleterious effect of anti-nepotism policies on women has been recognized, and there has been a decrease in the number of institutions which maintain them. In 1976, there were nine percent fewer institutions with these policies than in 1970, and 19 percent fewer than in 1960. While private institutions are less likely to still have anti-nepotism policies, the decrease since 1960 has been more dramatic in public institutions (Howard 1978).

But research indicates that even when there is a decline in the percentage of institutions with formal anti-nepotism policies, the actual percentage of husbands and wives being hired may remain virtually unchanged. In 1970, 59 percent of the institutions responding to an A.A.U.W. survey had husband-wife teams in the same department, while in 1976, 58 percent did. Eighty-five percent of the institutions had husbands and wives in different departments in 1970, while only 70 percent did in 1976 (Howard).

There is a gap between change in policy and change in practice, with attitudes against hiring husbands and wives, in the same department at least, still remaining. This notion was supported by the results of one study, in which over a third of department chairs surveyed indicated that they would not hire qualified husband-wife teams, citing such potential disadvantages as difficulty in faculty evaluations, disruption from the couple's marital problems, and disproportionate influence by the couple (Pingree et al. 1978). While the policies and the attitudes are not expressly directed against women, the practice in effect has been, as husbands are more likely than wives to be valued by institutions. Regardless of the intent and the possibility that it may indeed be preferable not to have family members in the same department, the effect has been to remove a large segment of well-qualified women from consideration for positions of status and reward.

The same is true for institutional policies regarding childbearing and child care. An institution may simply not address the whole area, saying that decisions regarding parenthood rest within the family, and therefore that solutions regarding its dilemmas should be personal and individual. However, as objective as this may seem on the surface, in reality, women are penalized far more than are men. Roles within families are generally constructed so that women assume primary responsibility for the care of children. This is even more true for single parents. The far larger portion of time and effort given to the care of children is given by women. For institutions to absolve themselves of responsibility in this area means that, in effect, they are creating an advantage for one sex over the other, and then are penalizing the disadvantaged group for not being able to develop solutions to equalize the balance.

Some faculty women with children have always been able to go to sympathetic department chairs to negotiate for some special allowances. Yet in having each case handled so individually, it may give the impression to both parties that the woman is asking for something quite out of the ordinary and a bit excessive, which is being granted only through the kindness and generosity of the department chair. One faculty member described asking for leave:

> My department chairman is very gentlemanly. When I came in and said, "I'm pregnant," he gave me time off. I

was very nervous about it—to come into a department and say, "I can't teach this semester," and presenting this problem. I felt as if none of the other men are coming in and presenting this problem, and I felt very badly that I had to say that and it felt as if I was asking for something unreasonable. I thought he was very chivalrous.

This would be equally or more true for faculty males asking for child care leave. Without an institutional structure to support the meshing of family and career for both faculty men and women, the combination does not become legitimized. As a result, the burden of finding a solution each time is placed on the individuals involved, and can be dependent on the attitudes, sympathies, favors, or "chivalry" of others. History is clear in showing that the sacrifices have been made more heavily, if not exclusively, by women.

The A.A.U.W. survey shows that from 1970-76, the percentage of institutions having childbearing leave available to faculty women increased from 70 percent to 86 percent. However, there was a 10 percent decline in the number of institutions which continued fringe benefits during leave. Institutions seem less supportive of the notion of childrearing leave, with 12 percent allowing it for women only, and 17 percent allowing it for men and women, in 1976 (Howard).

Another way in which institutions can support the successful combination of career and family is by providing adequate day care facilities for young children. Many institutions do provide some day care for the children of people affiliated with the institution. Yet again, the issue of child care may be perceived as being the individual problem of each individual family, or more likely, each individual woman. An attitude survey of assistant professors at the University of Rochester in 1975 showed that 92 percent of the women, but only 58 percent of the men felt that there should be more day care, while 14 percent of the men and none of the women felt strongly that there should not be (Glenwick et al. 1978). While taken from only a small sample, the results support the notion that men are far less likely to see child care as an institutional responsibility. One could speculate that this stems from the fact that they are less likely to be responsible for it. Nevertheless, as men are, at this point, the ones more likely to be in a policy-making capacity, these attitudes are reflected in the policies and services of the institutions. Institutions can and should play a major role in creating and maintaining supports for women in their role as parents. For institutions to fail to do so, perhaps claiming that these functions are the sole province of the family, means that they are creating structures which systematically favor one sex over the other.

The vast weight of the research shows that there is a basic incompatibility between married life and academic life for women, both in Jessie Bernard's time and today. Compared to men, academic women are significantly more likely to be never-married or divorced, to report less stable marriages, to have fewer children, and to see their families as detriments in some ways to their careers. For those academic women who are married, they are more likely to be working or studying part-time, to hold lower rank, or to be unemployed or employed in a job unrelated to their training.

One must wonder why this is so. Certainly on the face of it, one might assume that the flexible work schedule of faculty would be ideal for someone who wanted to devote time to a family.

Time may, however, be one of the pivotal factors. What may seem to others as a preponderance of free time should in fact be used for the solitary activities of thinking, reading, and writing for a faculty member to achieve professional success. Faculty men with families may be more able to do so, not only because they have fewer domestic demands on their time, but also because their home lives are constructed in such a way as to support these scholarly activities. Wives may offer direct intellectual, research, editorial, or clerical support, or at least ensure that their husbands have a quiet, solitary place to work, free of distractions. This is less likely to be true for academic women. Not only are they more likely to have more clear-cut demands on their time at home, but they are less likely to have the same types and amount of support from family.

Not only are married faculty women less likely to receive the same kinds of active support as are faculty men, they also may be more likely to receive hostility from husbands and other kin regarding their careers. This is suggested in one study by the higher divorce rate of women who were married before starting graduate school, and by the fact that those who remarried chose a mate more supportive of their career (Centra). It suggests that marriages have a difficult time surviving a radical change in status and role of the wife, and that supportiveness of the potential husband is a factor in a woman's decision to remarry. Nearly all of the authors note the importance of the husband's participation in nontraditional domestic arrangements in the potential success of married faculty women in their careers.

A compelling reason for the lower percentage of married women among the faculty ranks may be that those who are married are more likely to be sifted out along the way. One may be unable or unwilling to move to a distant location to accept a job offer. Another may interrupt her career to raise children, and then find it difficult five years later to pick up where she left off. Another may be denied fellowship support because she is perceived to not need it. Another may be unable to obtain a position at her husband's institution, or to find adequate day care in the surrounding area. Another may be unwilling to make the huge personal sacrifices necessary to juggle career and family, or is unable to find time to improve her publication record and is subsequently denied tenure. One by one, these women, in a Darwinian process of survival of the fittest, are eliminated from the profession. While men certainly undergo harsh competition in their race up the academic hierarchy, they are far less likely to be constrained by any or all of the factors listed above. Additionally, these factors are not the random, coincidental misfortunes which may or may not affect an individual, but rather are the direct result of the assumptions, attitudes, and policies which form the basis of institutions and families within American society. Thus, the lower representation of married women within the faculty ranks may not be wholly the result of choices made by women within that group, but rather the elimination from that group of women who have made these choices.

This systematic disadvantage for married women and relative advantage for married men is rarely taken into account in the assessment of the performance of individuals, or of both groups. While much writing does acknowledge the added burden married women face, it ultimately equates their lower status with personal deficiencies, such as their own inability to cope or a lack of motivation. For married men, however, there is rarely a mention of the institutionalized supports they receive. The implication that marital status is irrelevant in the success of married men does not acknowledge the various types of support academic men receive from their wives in the pursuit of their careers, nor does it recognize the ways in which institutional systems are based in traditionally male models of family/career interaction. This suggests that men succeed entirely on their own, and ignores the ways in which they are several steps ahead even before the race has begun. Certainly, the research shows that being married is highly related to success for married men.

Faculty women are further penalized by the perceptions of others regarding their marital status. Both married and single status are mixed blessings with regard to the attitudes and behavior of others. Married women may be seen by men as more "normal" and as more sexually safe, and thus more comfortable to interact with, yet they may also be taken less seriously and seen as less dedicated, ambitious, or mobile. Single women, whether lesbian or heterosexual, may be seen by men as more serious professional competition, but they may be threatening and confusing because they have seemingly rejected their most important gender-linked roles. Either result could have clear implications for women's careers. Regardless of a woman's marital status, it is likely to have an impact on the way in which she is seen and treated.

Despite all of the above-mentioned forms of discrimination, the burden has always been on the academic woman to create personal solutions to cope with them, and the blame has always fallen on her if she was unable to do so. However, despite the expectation that it is up to individual solutions, women are often penalized for those solutions they undertake. This is most notable for women who decide to work part-time when their children are young. These women are often underpaid, ineligible for tenure, seen as uncommitted and not worth investing in, burdened by large, undesirable introductory courses, and without power, status, or job security. While some paint the picture of "bored housewives" eager for part-time work to keep busy, recent legal and political action taken by women in this group suggests that their situation is less of their choosing and more a case of institutional exploitation.

Institutions do have a role and a responsibility in creating environments and policies which are supportive of women's attempts to combine career and family. Of course, as in any situation, the individuals directly involved must decide how they will cope with the challenges before them. But it is unfair that the environment in which these decisions are made is systematically advantageous to one sex over the other.

It is in this way that sexism takes its most insidious form, by being so woven into the fabric of institutional values, attitudes, assumptions, policies, and procedures that it becomes difficult to detect. Actions may seem to be a logical, objective response when in fact their outcomes are heavily biased in favor of men, the more obvious examples including anti-nepotism policies and the absence of day care facilities. It is no accident, for example, that the vast majority of institutions do not offer childrearing leave to men. Rather, it reflects the institutional value that it is unnecessary to do so, and perhaps even inappropriate for men to play that role. It is in this way that institutions perpetuate male-dominant values, while maintaining an appearance of objectivity and fairness. Institutional support for men and women trying to find non-traditional ways to mesh their families and careers legitimizes and rewards their efforts.

In a sense, there is something problematic about seeing the family/career issue as a woman's issue. To do so implies that care for the family is legitimately the women's role, and that the only problem is to give her assistance in carrying it out, putting responsibility for a solution on the victim, rather than the perpetrator. On the other hand, at the present time, women are far more likely than men to experience conflict between family and career as they are more likely to have family responsibilities, which are presumed "personal." They are far more likely to be disadvantaged by the impact of their marital status. Most married women, including the highly successful ones in nontraditional marriages interviewed for this study, seem to feel more responsible than do their husbands for the care of their families and for the active support of their spouses' career.

This situation has improved somewhat over the past two decades. Federal and state regulations prohibit discrimination on the basis of sex within programs and institutions receiving funding. There has been a sharp decline in the percentage of institutions having anti-nepotism policies. Childbearing and childrearing leave and day care are becoming more widespread. Women in part-time positions are beginning to receive more equitable compensation and status. Some institutions are even hiring husbands and wives to share positions.

However, while there has been progress in the formal policies and programs, attitudes and practice still lag behind. A basic incompatibility continues to exist between marriage and academic life for women. This is reflected in the startlingly low percentage of married women in academia and in the generally lesser professional success that these women have achieved. Only after institutions take an active role in creating systems which are as attuned to the lives of women as they are to the lives of men, and which support a wide variety of adaptations and living options, will this disparity cease to exist.

Conclusion

The research of the past two decades indicates clearly that those forces which dominated the careers of academic women in 1964 are still present today. While there has certainly been some improvement in the conditions they face, the overall picture remains basically unchanged.

This is exacerbated by a national political scene which appears hostile to the struggle for equity by women and other minorities, and a general societal notion that equality for women has been achieved. The feminist movement is frequently depicted in the press as dead.

Within academia, institutions are faced with shrinking enrollments and finances. In many fields, faculty jobs are difficult to obtain; at some schools, there have been such deep cutbacks that even tenured faculty are being dismissed. As women tend to be more heavily represented at the lower end of the spectrum, they may have been disproportionately affected by these problems. Their hold on the academic ladder may become even more tenuous in this environment of greater insecurity for everyone.

One positive measure is that both governmental and educational institutions have begun to take some steps to respond to the issue of discrimination. While enforcement of affirmative action regulations has been sporadic at best, the very existence of these laws has served as a threat which has motivated institutions to be more active in seeking out women and to be more fair in their treatment of them.

There also seems to be more institutional support for faculty women. Most of the policies which directly discriminated against

141

women have been eliminated, and institutions have begun to take steps to evaluate and eliminate those policies and practices which have outcomes detrimental to women, such as anti-nepotism regulations, absence of day care, and lack of childbearing and child-rearing leave. There is a greater awareness of the impact of sexual harassment on women faculty and students, and policies and grievance procedures have been instituted by many schools.

One reason for this has been the organized efforts of women faculty. An important and exciting change since Bernard's time has been the formation, strengthening, and acknowledgement of informal relationships among women faculty, for intellectual, political, professional, and emotional support. These networks have also served to support and encourage feminist scholarship and women's studies. While the inclusion of women is by no means an accepted part of the mainstream of research or curriculum, women doing and teaching feminist scholarship no longer represent a voice crying out in the wilderness. Within many disciplines, there is a healthy and energetic school of feminist thought. In conjunction with these efforts, women's associations, presses, journals, research centers, and other resources have begun and expanded. Women have supported each other's work to the point where it has gained some visibility and legitimacy.

In addition to producing and promoting feminist scholarship, networks of women have also played a vital and often solitary role in describing the forms that sexism takes within academia, and creating pressure for change. This has been true both nationally and within individual institutions. Despite traditional judicial reluctance to intervene in academic decision-making processes, there have been a number of successful lawsuits and grievances filed by women regarding decisions on promotion, tenure, salary, benefits, and other employment issues.

In all respects, women have benefitted from their professional relationships with each other. As important as the official associations are the informal relationships and networks formed among women within departments, institutions, disciplines, and academia in general. It is clear from the first-person accounts of faculty women, including those interviewed for this study, that they feel less vulnerable and more powerful when these informal networks operate in their lives.

It should not be fogotten, however, that despite the efforts women have made and the battles they have fought and won, academic women must still overcome the individual and institutional sexism that is woven into the fabric of academic life. For the average faculty woman, sexism can create innumerable subtle and blatant barriers to their progress. This discrimination takes two forms—individual and institutional. While the two are related, they manifest themselves in different ways.

Individual women are often the victims of anti-female attitudes and behavior on the part of others. The research indicates that today, as in Bernard's time, women are more likely to:

1) be seen by academic men as less serious and dedicated;
2) have less time devoted to their development by senior faculty;
3) be encouraged to enter certain fields, and discouraged from entering others;
4) have their work evaluated less positively than it deserves;
5) be seen and treated according to stereotypical roles;
6) be excluded from informal relationships with male colleagues and superiors.

These acts cannot merely be seen in isolation, as separate and discrete acts of prejudice. Because the vast majority of those in decision-making positions are male, systems are formed which conform more closely to the needs and experiences of academic men than women, particularly with regard to marital and family status. One cannot absolve academia of sexist discrimination when it is manifested in the acts of individuals, for those acts are reinforced by the assumptions, policies, and practices of the institutions themselves.

The research demonstrates clearly that on the whole, institutional systems have outcomes which are less favorable to women then to men. More specifically:

1) Despite evidence of stronger records of academic achievement and ability, faculty women are more likely than men to be unemployed, hold part-time or non-tenure track positions, be untenured, have lower salaries, and hold lower rank;
2) Women are represented in lowest proportions at the top colleges and universities, and have their highest representation at two year schools and small, less competitive, teaching-oriented colleges;

3) Women are more likely to be found in the less-valued and less-rewarded teaching role than in the role of researcher and scholar;

4) Childbearing and childrearing leave policies are such that it is difficult for women to integrate family and career;

5) Anti-nepotism practices prevent academic women who are also the wives of faculty men from receiving full-time appointments;

6) The contents of disciplines are structured around male perspectives, experiences, and contributions, with research on women seen as less valuable and important.

It will not be until institutions make sincere and far-reaching efforts to combat the sexism within their structures that women will be able to achieve true equity with men. Until that time, the commonly accepted notion of academia as a meritocracy will simply be untrue.

Thus, despite the perception of sweeping changes and dramatic progress, the status of academic women has not improved substantially since Jessie Bernard published *Academic Women* in 1964. However, there is evidence to indicate that the situation is more hopeful than the statistics may suggest. While the injustices may not have changed, women's responses to them have. On virtually every dimension, there are concerted efforts to correct inequities and create supports for women. More and more women are coming through the academic pipeline, which will inevitably make their voices more difficult to ignore. Even within a more conservative social climate, it is difficult to imagine that their efforts will dissolve and their gains will disappear.

After approximately 150 years of participation in higher education, women still have not nearly achieved a position of equity. But, the past two decades have perhaps given them cause for hope rather than despair. In a 1982 address at a women's studies conference, while discussing the status of women around the world, Bernard described herself as someone who sees the water glass as being half-full, rather than half-empty. Perhaps her optimism is justified in the sense that the community of women within academia is a vibrant, exciting, and growing one. While the changes have not been great, the potential for change has grown enormously. One can only hope that two decades hence, that potential will have been realized.

Bibliography

Abel, Elizabeth, and Abel, Emily (eds.). 1983. *The Signs Reader: Women, Gender and Scholarship.* Chicago: University of Chicago Press.

Abramson, Joan. 1975. *The Invisible Woman.* San Francisco: Jossey-Bass Publishers.

Acker, Sandra. 1977. "Sex Differentials in Graduate Student Ambition. Do Men Publish While Women Perish?" *Sex Roles* 3: 285-299.

Adler, Nancy. 1976. "Women Students." In *Scholars in the Making,* Joseph Katz and Rodney T. Hartnett, eds. Cambridge, Mass.: Ballinger Publishing Company, pp. 197-227.

American Association of University Professors (A.A.U.P.) 1983. "Sexual Harassment: Suggested Policy and Procedures for Handling Complaints." *Academe* (March-April): 15a-16a.

————. 1982. Cited in "Nine Month Salaries for 1981-82." *Chronicle of Higher Education* (7 July): 10.

Andruskiw, Olga, and Howe, Nancy J. 1980. "Dispelling a Myth that Stereotypic Attitudes Influence Evaluation of Women as Administrators in Higher Education." *Journal of Higher Education* 51: 475-496.

Astin, Helen S. 1969. *The Woman Doctorate in America.* New York: Russell Sage Foundation.

Astin, Helen S., and Bayer, Alan E. 1979. "Pervasive Sex Differences in the Academic Reward System: Scholarship, Marriage, and What Else?" In *Academic Rewards in Higher Education,* Darrell R. Lewis and William E. Becker, Jr. eds. Cambridge, Mass.: Ballinger Publishing Company, pp. 211- 229.

Astin, Helen S., and Snyder, Mary Beth. 1982. "A Decade of Response." *Change* 14: 26-31, 59.

145

Baird, Leonard L. 1976. "Who Goes to Graduate School and How They Get There." In *Scholars in the Making*, Joseph Katz and Rodney T. Hartnett, eds. Cambridge, Mass.: Ballinger Publishing Company, pp. 19-48.

Bernard, Jessie. 1974. *Academic Women*. University Park, Pennsylvania: The Pennsylvania State University Press, 1964; reprint ed., New York: New American Library.

———— 1982. "Benchmark for the 80's." In *Handbook for Women Scholars*, Mary Spencer, Monika Kehoe, and Karen Speece, eds. San Francisco: Americas Behavioral Research Corporation, pp. 69-80.

Blackburn, Robert T., Chapman, David W., and Cameron, Susan M. 1981. "Cloning in Academe: Mentorship and Academic Careers." *Research in Higher Education* 5: 315-327.

Bonham, Goerge W. (ed.) 1975. *Women on Campus: The Unfinished Liberation*. New Rochelle, New York: Change Magazine.

Boxer, Marilyn, J. 1982. "For and About Women: The Theory and Practice of Women's Studies in the United States." *Signs* 7: 661-695.

Bryan, Alice I., and Boring, Edwin G. 1947. "Women in American Psychology: Factors Affecting Their Professional Careers." *American Psychologist* 5: 10-19.

Bryson, Rebecca, Bryson, Jeff B., and Johnson, Marilyn F. 1978. "Family Size, Satisfaction, and Productivity in Dual Career Families." *Psychology of Women Quarterly* 3: 67-77.

Centra, John A. 1974. *Women, Men and the Doctorate*. Princeton: Educational Testing Service.

Childers, Karen, Rackin, Phyllis, Secor, Cynthia, and Tracy, Carol. 1981. "A Network of One's Own." In *Rocking the Boat: Academic Women and Academic Processes*, Gloria De Sole and Leonore Hoffman, eds. New York: Modern Language Association of America.

Cole, Jonathan R. 1979. *Fair Science: Women in the Scientific Community*. New York: The Free Press.

Committee on the Education and Employment of Women in Science and Engineering. 1979. *Climbing the Academic Ladder: Doctoral Women Scientists in Academe*. Washington, D.C.: National Academy of Sciences.

————. 1983. *Climbing the Ladder: An Update on the Status of Doctoral Women Scientists and Engineers*. Washington, D.C.: National Academy Press.

Cowan, Alison Leigh. 1983. "Female Professors Fear U.S. in Retreat on Bias Cases." *New York Times*, 13 November, sec. 12, p. 17.

Crocker, Phyllis L. 1983. "An Analysis of University Definitions of Sexual Harassment." *Signs* 8: 699.

Cruikshank, Margaret, (ed.). 1982. *Lesbian Studies: Present and Future.* New York: The Feminist Press.

Davenport, Doris. 1982. "Black Lesbians in Academia: Visible Invisibility." In *Lesbian Studies: Present and Future,"* Margaret Cruikshank, ed. New York: The Feminist Press, pp. 9-12.

Deglar, Carl N. 1982. "What the Women's Movement Has Done to American History." In *A Feminist Perspective in the Academy: The Difference It Makes,* Elizabeth Langland and Walter Grove, eds. Chicago: University of Chicago Press, pp. 67-85.

Delphy, Christine. 1981. "Women in Stratification Studies." In *Doing Feminist Research,* Helen Roberts ed. London: Routledge and Kegan Paul, pp. 114-128.

DeReimer, Cynthia, Quarles, Dan R., and Temple, Charles M. 1982. "The Success Rate of Personal Salary Negotiations: A Further Investigation of Academic Pay Differentials by Sex." *Research in Higher Education* 16: 139-154.

Desrusseaux, Paul. 1984. "Federal Judge Upholds Women's Claim of Salary Discrimination at C.U.N.Y." *Chronicle of Higher Education* (29 Feb.): 10.

De Sole, Gloria, and Hoffman, Leonore (eds.). 1981. *Rocking the Boat: Academic Women and Academic Processes.* New York: Modern Language Association of America.

DuBois, Ellen Carol, Kelly, G. P., Kennedy, E. L., Korsmeyer, C.W., and Robinson, L.S. (eds.). 1985. *Feminist Scholarship: Kindling in the Groves of Academe.* Urbana, Illinois: University of Illinois Press.

Dzeich, Billie Wright and Weiner, Linda. 1984. *The Lecherous Professor: Sexual Harassment on Campus.* Boston: Beacon Press.

Eckert, Ruth, and Stecklein, J.E. 1961. *Job Motivation and Satisfaction of College Teachers: A Study of Faculty Members in Minnesota Colleges.* Washington, D.C.: Government Printing Office.

El-Khawas, Elaine H., and Bisconti, Ann S. 1974. *Five and Ten Years After College Entry.* Washington, D.C.: American College on Education.

Etaugh, Claire, and Kasley, Helen Czachorski. 1981. "Evaluating Competence: Effects of Sex, Marital Status and Parental Status." *Psychology of Women Quarterly* 6: 196-203.

Farber, Stephen. 1977. "The Earnings and Promotion of Women Faculty." *American Economic Review* 67: 199-206.

Feldman, Saul D. 1974. *Escape from the Doll's House: Women in Graduate and Professional School Education.* New York: McGraw-Hill.

Field, Jewel Cardwell. 1961. "Factors Associated with Graduate School Attendance and Role Definition of the Women Doctoral Candidates at the Pennsylvania State University." M.A. thesis, Pennsylvania State University.

Fields, Cheryl M. 1982. "Title IX at X." *Chronicle of Higher Education* (23 June): 1, 12.

———. 1984a. "Appeals Court Rejects Sex-Bias Charges by Four Former Cornell Professors," *Chronicle of Higher Education* (29 Feb.): 10.

———. 1984b. "New Ruling Said to Make Job Bias Harder to Prove," *Chronicle of Higher Education* (1 Aug.): 1, 19.

Freeman, Bonnie Cook. 1977. "Faculty Women in the American University: Up the Down Staircase." *Higher Education* 6: 165-188.

Gilligan, Carol. 1982. In *A Different Voice: Psychological Theory and Women's Development*. Cambridge, Massachusetts: Harvard University Press.

Glenwick, David S., Johanson, Sandra L., Bondy, Jeffrey. 1978. "A Comparison of the Self-Images of Female and Male Assistant Professors." *Sex Roles* 4: 513-524.

Goldstein, Elyse. 1979. "Effects of Same-sex and Cross-sex Role Models on the Subsequent Academic Productivity of Scholars." *American Psychologist* (May): 407-409.

Goode, William J. 1982. "Why Men Resist." In *Rethinking the Family*, Barrie Thorne, ed. New York: Longman.

Gornick, Vivian. 1983. *Women in Science: Portraits from a World in Transition*. New York: Simon and Schuster.

Gropper, George Leonard, and Fitzpatrick, Robert. 1959. *Who Goes to Graduate School?* Pittsburgh: American Institute for Research.

Hall, Roberta M., and Sandler, Bernice R. 1983. *Academic Mentoring for Women Students and Faculty: A New Look at an Old Way to Get Ahead*. Washington, D.C.: Project on the Status and Education of Women, Association of American Colleges.

Hallon, Charles J., and Gemmill, Gary R. 1976. "A Comparison of Female and Male Professors on Participation in Decision- Making, Job-related Tension, Job Involvement, and Job Satisfaction." *Education Administration Quarterly* 12: 80- 93.

Hamovitch, William, and Morganstern, Richard D. 1977. "Children and the Productivity of Academic Women." *Journal of Higher Education* 48: 633-645.

Harmon, Lindsey R., and Soldz, Herbert. 1963. *Doctorate Production in United States Universities 1920-1962*. Washington, D.C.: National Academy of Sciences- National Research Council.

Harmon, Lindsey R. 1961. "The High School Backgrounds of Science Doctorates." *Science* (March 10): 679-688.

Hartnett, Rodney T. 1976. "Environments for Advanced Learning." In *Scholars in the Making*, Joseph Katz and Rodney T. Hartnett, eds. Cambridge, Mass.: Ballinger Publishing Company, pp. 49-84.

Hochschild, Arlie Russell. 1975. "Inside the Clockwork of Male Careers." In *Women and the Power to Change*, Florence Howe, ed. New York: McGraw-Hill, pp. 47-80.

Hoffman, Emily. 1976. "Faculty Salaries: Is There Discrimination by Sex, Race, and Disciplines? Additional Evidence." *American Economic Review* 66: 196-198.

Holahan, Carole Kovalic. 1979. "Stress Experienced by Women Doctoral Students, Need for Support, and Occupational Sex Typing: An Interactional View." *Sex Roles* 5: 425-436.

Howard, Suzanne. 1978. *But We Will Persist.* Washington, D.C.: American Association of University Women.

Howe, Florence (ed.). 1975. *Women and the Power to Change.* New York: McGraw-Hill.

Hull, Gloria T., Scott, Patricia Bell, and Smith, Barbara, (eds.). 1982. *But Some of Us Are Brave: Black Women's Studies.* Old Westbury, New York: The Feminist Press.

Isaacs, Marla Beth. 1981. "Sex Role Stereotyping and the Evaluation of the Performance of Women: Changing Trends." *Psychology of Women Quarterly* 6: 187-195.

Jacobson, Paul H. 1959. *American Marriage and Divorce.* New York: Rinehart.

Jencks, Christopher, and Riesman, David. 1968. *The Academic Revolution.* Chicago: University of Chicago Press.

Jensen, Katherine. 1982. "Women's Work and Academic Culture: Adaptations and Confrontations." *Higher Education* 11: 67-83.

Johnson, George E., and Stafford, Frank E. 1979. "Pecuniary Rewards to Men and Women Faculty." In *Academic Rewards in Higher Education*, Darrell R. Lewis and William E. Becker, Jr., eds. Cambridge, Mass.: Ballinger Publishing Company, pp. 231-243.

――――― .1974. "Earnings and Promotion of Faculty Women." *American Economic Review* 64: 888-903.

Kanter, Rosabeth Moss. 1977. *Men and Women of the Corporation.* New York: Basic Books.

Kaschak, Ellyn. 1978. "Sex Bias in Student Evaluations of College Professors." *Psychology of Women Quarterly* 2: 235-243.

Katz, Joseph, and Hartnett, Rodney T., (eds.) *Scholars in the Making.* Cambridge, Mass.: Ballinger Publishing Company, 1976.

Kaufman, Debra Renee. 1978. "Associational Ties in Academe: Some Male and Female Differences." *Sex Roles* 4: 9-21.

Keller, Evelyn Fox. 1983. "Feminism and Science." In *The Signs Reader: Women, Gender and Scholarship,* Elizabeth Abel and Emily K. Abel, eds. Chicago: University of Chicago Press, pp. 109-122.

Keohane, Nannerl O. 1982. "Speaking from Silence: Women of Politics." In *A Feminist Perspective in the Academy: The Difference it Makes,* Elizabeth Langland and Walter Gove, eds. Chicago: University of Chicago Press, pp. 86-100.

Langland, Elizabeth, and Gove, Walter (eds.). 1982. *A Feminist Perspective in the Academy: The Difference It Makes.* Chicago: University of Chicago Press.

Laws, Judith Long. 1975. "The Psychology of Tokenism: An Analysis." *Sex Roles* 1: 51-67.

Lester, Richard A. 1975. "The Equal Pay Boondoggle." *Change* 7: 38-43.

Lewis, Darrell R., and Becker, William E. Jr. (eds.). 1979. *Academic Rewards in Higher Education.* Cambridge, Mass.: Ballinger Publishing Company.

Lewis, Lionel S. 1975. *Scaling the Ivory Tower: Merit and Its Limits in Academic Careers.* Baltimore: Johns Hopkins University Press.

Lewis-Beck, J. Arline. 1980. "The Participation of Men and Women in Educational Research: Another Look." *Sex Roles* 6: 607-610.

Lieberman, Marcia R. 1981. "The Most Important Thing for You to Know." In *Rocking the Boat: Academic Women and Academic Processes,* Gloria DeSole and Lenore Hoffman, eds. New York: Modern Language Association of America, pp. 3-7.

Lovenduski, Joni. 1981. "Toward the Emasculation of Political Science: The Impact of Feminism." In *Men's Studies Modified: The Impact of Feminism on the Academic Disciplines,* Dale Spender, ed. Oxford: Pergamon Press, pp. 83-98.

Mackie, Marlene. 1977. "Professional Women's Collegial Relations and Productivity: Female Sociologists' Journal Publications, 1967 and 1973." *Sociology and Social Research* 61: 277-293.

Martin, Elaine. 1984. "Power and Authority in the Classroom: Sexist Stereotypes in Teaching Evaluations." *Signs* 9: 482-492.

Maxfield, Betty D., Ahern, Nancy C., and Spisak, Andrew W. 1976. *Employment Status of Ph.D. Scientists and Engineers, 1973 and 1975.* Washington, D.C.: National Academy of Sciences.

McCain, Nina. 1983. "Female Faculty Members and Students at Harvard Report Sexual Harassment." *Chronicle of Higher Education* (2 Nov.): 1.

Menges, Robert J. and Exum, William H. 1983. "Barriers to Progress of Women and Minority Faculty." *Journal of Higher Education* 54: 123-144.

Miller, Jean Baker. 1976. *Toward a New Psychology of Women*. Boston, Mass.: Beacon Press.

Mokros, Janice R., Erkut, Sumru, and Spichiger, Lynne. 1981. *Mentoring and Being Mentored: Sex-related Patterns among College Professors*. Wellesley, Mass.: Wellesley College Center for Research on Women.

Moore, Kathryn M. 1982. "The Role of Mentors in Developing Leaders for Academe." *Educational Record* 63: 23-28.

National Center for Education Statistics. 1984. Cited in "National Averages for 1982-83 Salaries." *Chronicle of Higher Education* (8 Feb.): 21.

―――. 1982. Cited in "Enrollment Last Fall: Up 2.3 Percent." *Chronicle of Higher Education* (14 July): 10.

―――. 1982. Cited in "Trends in Higher Education: Enrollment, Staff, and Degrees in 50 States and D.C." *Chronicle of Higher Education* (23 June): 10.

―――. 1978-81. *The Condition of Education*. Washington, D.C.: U.S. Government Printing Office.

National Education Association (N.E.A.). 1960. *Salaries Paid and Salary Practices in Universities, Colleges and Junior Colleges, 1959-1960*. Washington, D.C.: National Education Association.

National Research Council, Commission on Human Resources. 1977. *Personnel Needs and Training for Biomedical and Behavioral Research—1977 Report, Vol. II*. Washington, D.C.: National Academy of Sciences.

National Research Council (N.R.C.). 1982. *Survey of Earned Doctorates*. Cited in "A Profile of 1980-81 Recipients of Doctorates." *Chronicle of Higher Education* (6 Oct.): 8.

National Research Council (N.R.C.). 1977. *Survey of Earned Doctorates Awarded in the United States*. Washington, D.C.

National Science Foundation (N.S.F.). 1961. *Women in Scientific Careers*. Washington, D.C.: Government Printing Office.

―――. 1984. *Women and Minorities in Science and Engineering*. Washington, D.C.: National Science Foundation.

Office of Education. 1958. *Statistics of Higher Education 1955-56: Faculty, Students and Degrees*. Washington, D.C.: Government Printing Office.

————. 1961. *Summary Report on Faculty and other Professional Staff in Institutions of Higher Education, 1959-60.* Washington, D.C.: Government Printing Office.

————. 1962. *Earned Degrees Conferred, 1959-60.* Washington, D.C.: Government Printing Office.

————. 1963. *Summary Report on Faculty and Other Professional Staff in Institutions of Higher Education, 1961-62.* Washington, D.C.: Government Printing Office.

Oakley, Ann. 1981. "Interviewing Women: A Contradiction in Terms." In *Doing Feminist Research,* Helen Roberts, ed. London: Routledge and Kegan Paul, pp. 30-61.

Parrish, John B. 1962. "Women in Top Level Teaching and Research." *Journal of American Association of University Women* 55: 100-110.

Peck, Teresa. 1978. "When Women Evaluate Women, Nothing Succeeds Like Success: The Differential Effects of Status upon Evaluations of Male and Female Professional Ability." *Sex Roles* 4: 205-213.

Perry, Suzanne. 1983. "Sex Bias in Academe: A Sweeping Decree Helps Minnesota Women Press Claims." *Chronicle of Higher Education* (31 Aug.): 15-16.

Pezzullo, Thomas R. and Brittingham, Barbara E. (eds.). 1979. *Salary Equity.* Lexington, Mass.: D.C. Heath and Company.

Pingree, Suzanne, Butler, Matilda, Paisley, William, and Hawkins, Robert. 1978. "Anti-Nepotism's Ghost: Attitudes of Administrators Toward Hiring Professional Couples." *Psychology of Women Quarterly* 3: 22-29.

Polakoff, Sally E. 1984. "A Plan for Coping with Sexual Harassment." *Journal of College Student Personnel* (March): 165-167.

Prescott, Suzanne. 1978. "Why Researchers Don't Study Women: The Response of 62 Researchers." *Sex Roles* 4: 899-906.

"Report of the Committee to Survey Sexual Harassment at the University of Pennsylvania." 1985. *Almanac Supplement* (24 Sept.): i-xii.

Rich, Adrienne. 1975. "Toward a Woman-Centered University." In *Women and the Power to Change,* Florence Howe, ed. New York: McGraw-Hill, pp. 15-46.

Rivers, Caryl, Barnett, Rosalind, and Baruch, Grace. 1979. *Beyond Sugar and Spice: How Women Grow, Learn and Thrive.* New York: G.P. Putnam's Sons.

Roberts, Helen. 1981. "Women and their Doctors: Power and Powerlessness in the Research Process." In *Doing Feminist Research,* Helen Roberts, ed. London: Routledge and Kegan Paul.

Roberts, Helen (ed.). 1981. *Doing Feminist Research.* London: Routledge and Kegan Paul.

Robertson, Diane. 1979. "Women Business School Academicians: Disparities and Progress." *Sex Roles* 5: 635-647.

Rorty, Amelia Oksenberg. 1977. "Dependency, Individuality, and Work." In *Working It Out: 23 Women Writers, Artists, Scientists and Scholars Talk About Their Lives and Work*, Sara Ruddick and Pamela Daniels, eds. New York: Pantheon Books, pp. 38-54.

Ruth, Sheila. 1981. "Methodocracy, Misogyny and Bad Faith: The Response of Philosophy." In *Men's Studies Modified: The Impact of Feminism on the Academic Disciplines*, Dale Spender, ed. Oxford: Pergamon Press, pp. 43-54.

Ruddick, Sara and Daniels, Pamela (eds.). 1977. *Working It Out: 23 Women Writers, Artists, Scientists, and Scholars Talk about their Lives and Work.* New York: Pantheon Books.

Sanger, David E. 1985. "Harvard Offers Tenure to Woman." *New York Times*, 8 January, sec. A, p. 11.

Schumer, Fran R. 1981. "A Question of Sex Bias at Harvard." *New York Times Magazine*, 18 October, pp. 96-104.

Scott, Patricia Bell. 1982. "Debunking Sapphire: Toward a Non- Racist and Non-Sexist Social Science." In *But Some of Us Are Brave: Black Women's Studies.*, Gloria T. Hull, Patricia Bell Scott, and Barbara Smith, eds. Old Westbury, New York: The Feminist Press, pp. 85-92.

Shapiro, Eileen. 1982. "A Survival Guide." In *Handbook for Women Scholars*, Mary L. Spencer, Monika Kehoe, and Karen Speece, eds. San Francisco: Americas Behavioral Research Corporation.

Shapiro, Joan, and Fitzgerald, Anne. 1982. "Women's Studies: Transformation of Curriculum and of Research." Unpublished manuscript.

Snow, C.P. 1959. *The Two Cultures and the Scientific Revolution.* New York: Cambridge University Press.

Solmon, Lewis C. 1976. *Male and Female Graduate Students: The Question of Equal Opportunity.* New York: Praeger Publishers.

———. 1973. "Women in Doctoral Education: Clues and Puzzles Regarding Institutional Discrimination." *Research in Higher Education* 1: 299-332.

Speizer, Jeanne J. 1981. "Role Models, Mentors, and Sponsors: The Ellusive Concepts." *Signs* 6: 692-712.

Spencer, Mary L., and Bradford, Eva. 1982. "Status and Needs of Women Scholars." In *Handbook for Women Scholars*, Mary L. Spencer, Monika Kehoe, and Karen Speece, eds. San Francisco: Americas Behavioral Research Corporation, pp. 3-30.

Spencer, Mary L., Kehoe, Monika, and Speece Karen (eds.). 1982. *Handbook for Women Scholars*. San Francisco: Americas Behavioral Research Corporation.

Spender, Dale (ed.). 1981. *Men's Studies Modified: The Impact of Feminism on the Academic Disciplines*. Oxford: Pergamon Press.

"Stanford Provost Approves Tenure for Feminist Scholar." 1983. *Chronicle of Higher Education* (27 July): 3.

Stitzel, Judith. 1982. "She Who Laughs First." In *Stepping Off the Pedestal" Academic Women in the South*, Patricia A. Stringer and Irene Thompson, eds. New York: Modern Language Association of America, pp. 130-134.

Stringer, Patricia A., and Thompson, Irene (eds.). 1982. *Stepping Off the Pedestal: Academic Women in the South*. New York: Modern Language Association of America.

Stroeber, Myra H., and Quester, Aline O. 1977. "The Earnings and Promotion of Women Faculty: Comment." *American Economic Review* 67: 207-213.

Tidball, Elizabeth. 1976. "Of Men and Research." *Journal of Higher Education* 47: 373-390.

———. 1975. "The Search for Talented Women." In *Women on Campus: The Unfinished Revolution*, George W. Bonham, ed. New Rochelle, New York: Change, pp. 152-159.

Thorne, Barrie. 1982. *Rethinking the Family*. New York: Longman.

Till, F.J. 1980. *Sexual Harassment: A report on the sexual harassment of students*. Washington, D.C.: National Advisory Council on Women's Educational Programs.

Tuckman, Barbara Hauber. 1979. "Salary Differences among University Faculty and their Implications for the Future." In *Salary Equity*, Thomas R. Pezzulla and Barbara E. Bittingham, eds. Lexington, Mass.: D.C. Heath and Company, pp. 19-38.

U.S. Department of Education Center for Statistics. 1986. Cited in "Women Flock to Graduate School in Record Numbers, but Fewer Blacks Are Entering the Academic Pipeline." 1986. *Chronicle of Higher Education* (10 Sept.): 1, 25.

Vetter, Betty M., and Babco, E. 1978. *Professional Women and Minorities*. Washington, D.C.: Scientific Manpower Commission.

Wallston, Barbara Strudler, Foster, Martha A., and Berger, Michelle. 1978. "I will follow him—Myth, Reality or Forced Choice—Job Seeking Experience of Dual-Career Couples." *Psychology of Women Quarterly* 3: 9-21.

Ward, Helene. 1960. American Association of University Women. Report.

Weisstein, Naomi. 1977. "'How Can a Little Girl Like You Teach a Great Big Class of Men?' the Chairman Said, and other Adventures of a Woman in Science." In *Working It Out: 23 Women Writers, Artists, Scientists and Scholars Talk about their Lives and Work*, Sara Ruddick and Pamela Daniels, eds. New York: Pantheon Books, pp. 241-250.

Widom, Cathy Spatz, and Burke, Barbara W. 1978. "Performance, Attitudes, and Professional Socialization of Women in Academia." *Sex Roles* 4: 549-562.

Williams, Dennis A., Zabarski, Martha, and McDonald, Dianne H. 1983. "Out of the Academic Ghetto." *Newsweek*, 31 Oct., p. 86.

Wilson, Logan. 1979. *American Academics: Then and Now.* New York: Oxford University Press.

Winkler, Karen J. 1983. "Feminist Professor v. Stanford: A Tenure Test Case." *Chronicle of Higher Education* (16 Feb.): 5.

"Women Chemists Mortality Study Finds High Suicide Rate." 1984. *Chemical and Engineering News*, 23 April, p. 1.

Young, Carlotta Joyner, Michenzie, Doris Layton, and Sherif, Carolyn Wood. 1980. "In Search of Token Women in Academia." *Psychology of Women Quarterly* 4: 508-525.

Index

Other Books of Interest from *Bergin & Garvey*

WOMEN TEACHING FOR CHANGE
GENDER, CLASS & POWER
KATHLEEN WEILER
Introduction by Henry A. Giroux & Paulo Freire
Critical Studies in Education Series
240 Pages

WOMEN'S WORK
Development & the Division of Labor by Gender
ELEANOR LEACOCK, HELEN I. SAFA & CONTRIBUTORS
304 Pages   Illustrations

WOMEN & CHANGE IN LATIN AMERICA
New Directions in Sex and Class
JUNE NASH, HELEN I. SAFA & CONTRIBUTORS
384 Pages   Illustrations

IN HER PRIME
A New View of Middle-Aged Women
JUDITH BROWN, VIRGINIA KERNS & CONTRIBUTORS
240 Pages   Illustrations

SILENT KNIFE
Cesarean Prevention & Vaginal Birth After Cesarean
NANCY WAINER COHEN & LOIS J. ESTNER
464 Pages   Illustrations

AMERICAN SOCIETY, Revised
The Welfare State & Beyond
JOSEPH BENSMAN & ARTHUR J. VIDICH
368 Pages

BERGIN & GARVEY PUBLISHERS, INC.
670 Amherst Road
South Hadley, MA 01075